PLANNING FOR FREEDOM:
LET THE MARKET SYSTEM WORK

LUDWIG VON MISES

Planning for Freedom:
Let the Market System Work
A Collection of Essays and Addresses

ᏨᎳ LUDWIG VON MISES

Edited and with a Foreword by Bettina Bien Greaves

LIBERTY FUND   *Indianapolis*

New foreword and editorial additions © 2008 by Liberty Fund, Inc.
Originally published as *Planning for Freedom and Other Essays and
Addresses* by Libertarian Press in 1952, 1962, and 1974. Published as
Planning for Freedom and Sixteen Other Essays and Addresses by
Libertarian Press in 1980.

Library of Congress Cataloging-in-Publication Data

Von Mises, Ludwig, 1881–1973.
    Planning for freedom: let the market system work: a collection of es-
says and addresses / Ludwig von Mises; edited by Bettina Bien Greaves.
        p.   cm—(Liberty Fund library of the works of Ludwig von Mises)
    "Liberty Fund edition."
    "New foreword and editorial additions"—T.p. verso.
    Rev. ed. Originally published in 1952 as: Planning for freedom and
other essays and addresses; and issued in 1980 as: Planning for freedom
and sixteen other essays and addresses.
    Includes bibliographical references and index.
    ISBN 978-0-86597-660-3 (hbk.: alk. paper)—ISBN 978-0-86597-661-0
(pbk.: alk. paper)   1. Economic policy.   I. Greaves, Bettina Bien.
II. Von Mises, Ludwig, 1881–1973. Planning for freedom, and sixteen
other essays and addresses.   III. Title.
    HD82.V6 2008
    330.12'2—dc22
                                                          2008001103

Liberty Fund, Inc.
8335 Allison Pointe Trail, Suite 300
Indianapolis, Indiana 46250-1684

CONTENTS

PART 4 Ideas

Foreword to the Liberty Fund Edition

In 1947, Ludwig von Mises received a letter from a complete stranger who had been reading Mises's book on money. One paragraph didn't make sense to him. He asked Mises for clarification. The letter writer was Fred C. Nymeyer, an Illinois businessman. In his reply, Mises complimented Nymeyer: His "thoroughness and critical acumen" in studying his book was "very flattering indeed for the author. You represent the unfortunately very rare type of discriminating readers for whom alone it is worthwhile to write books." [1] As a result of that exchange, Nymeyer and Mises soon met and became close friends.

Nymeyer believed the economic understanding he had gained from his study of Mises and the Austrian School of Economics had contributed to his success in business and he wanted to say thanks in some way. At Mises's suggestion, therefore, he published in 1951, as a monograph, "Profit and Loss," a paper Mises had given that year at the Beauvallon, France, meeting of the international free-enterprise Mont Pèlerin Society. Later when Nymeyer suggested putting out an anthology of several of Mises's papers, Mises asked that "Profit and Loss" be included. Thus, *Planning for Freedom* appeared in 1952 with "Profit and Loss" plus eleven other Mises essays and addresses undoubtedly selected by Mises himself. [2] A second edition of *Planning for Freedom*, enlarged by

1. When Mises checked the paragraph Nymeyer had questioned (p. 108 in the 1934 British translation), he discovered that the German original had indeed been misinterpreted. "Your criticism," he wrote Mr. Nymeyer, "is fully justified. . . . If a new edition of the English translation is made, I will alter the passage concerned so as to avoid confusion." A corrected translation of this paragraph has been made on pp. 129–130 of Liberty Fund's 2005 printing of their edition of *The Theory of Money and Credit*.

2. Mises suggested to Nymeyer later that the three-volume work *Kapital und Kapitalzins* by Mises's mentor and professor Eugen von Böhm–Bawerk should be translated into English in

the addition of a thirteenth essay, came out in 1962, followed by a third memorial edition (1974) and a fourth edition (1980), which reprinted four more Mises papers, bringing the total to seventeen. The later editions of this anthology, published after Mises's death in 1973, included also, as a tribute to Mises, various papers by other authors *about* him. As these additional materials have been covered in the burgeoning post–1980 Mises literature, they have been deleted here, making this edition of *Planning Freedom* a collection of Mises's writings exclusively. Further, the articles and papers in this edition have been rearranged by subject into four parts: "The Free Market Economy versus Government Planning," "Money, Inflation, and Government," "Mises: Critic of Inflationism and Socialism," and "Ideas."

Many changes have taken place in the world during the decades since these papers were written. The trend toward interventionism has been slowed in some countries, speeded up in others. Editor's notes have been introduced in this edition to explain some of these changes, as well as Mises's references to historical events.

Many of the papers in this collection were written as speeches. When addressing a one-time audience, Mises always chose his words carefully and precisely. He sought to make complex topics—inflation, price controls, capital investment, social security, unemployment, etc.—simple and easy for his listeners to understand.

For instance, on price controls, if the government imposes a ceiling on the price of milk because it considers its price too high and because it wants the poor to be able to give their children more milk, farmers whose costs are so high that they cannot stay in business and sell milk at the controlled price will stop producing milk and will produce butter, cheese, or meat instead. The result: less milk for poor children ("Middle-of-the-Road Policy Leads to Socialism," p. 43–44).

On market operations: "There is nothing automatic or mysterious in the operation of the market. The only forces determining the continually fluctuating state of the market are the value judgments of the various individuals and their actions as directed by these value judgments. . . . Supremacy of the market is tantamount to the supremacy of the consumers. By their buying and by their abstention from buying the

---

its entirety and final version. As a result Nymeyer financed its translation by Hans F. Sennholz, then a student at New York University working for a doctorate under Mises, and published it as *Capital and Interest* (Libertarian Press, 1959).

consumers determine not only the price structure, but no less what should be produced and in what quantity and quality and by whom. . . . They make poor men rich and rich men poor" ("Inflation and Price Control," p. 53–54).

When it comes to money, Mises rejected the imprecise definition of inflation as "higher prices." For him, "Nothing is inflationary except inflation, i.e., an increase in the quantity of money in circulation and credit subject to check (check-book money). And under present conditions nobody but the government can bring an inflation into being" ("Wages, Unemployment, and Inflation," p. 73).

"The inevitable result of inflationary policies is a drop in the monetary unit's purchasing power. . . . In an industrial society all deferred payments must be stipulated in terms of money. They shrink with the shrinking of the money's purchasing power. A policy of deficit spending [government spending in excess of income] saps the very foundation of all interpersonal relations and contracts. It frustrates all kinds of savings, social security benefits and pensions" ("Economic Aspects of the Pension Problem," p. 64–65).

The longest, and by far the most important, paper in this collection is "Profit and Loss." Mises was driven by the firm belief that the only way to save civilization and to promote peace and prosperity among nations was to change the ideas of the people. He fought to educate with the only weapons available to him—the spoken and written word. He did his best to explain free market principles, capitalism, and the workings of the market economy. Clarity of expression was extremely important. When a student asked a question in class, Mises quite often urged him to write down his ideas—in Mises's view, the discipline of writing, of having to be precise, might very well help him answer his own question. Mises, of course, practiced what he preached; the books and articles he wrote are legion. In his magnum opus, *Human Action* (1949), Mises had written as precisely and as clearly as he could about all aspects of economics. Yet after publishing *Human Action*, Mises thought he could improve his explanation of profit and loss, so he took advantage of an opportunity to present a paper before the Mont Pelerin Society to explain still more fully entrepreneurial profits and losses. In that analysis, reprinted here, he destroys the Marxian theme that profits deprive laborers of their full share of production, that profits come from exploiting consumers, that profits are compensation for risk taking, management, or time. Successful entrepreneurs, Mises points out, actually create new wealth. They convert (transform, combine, refine, transport) raw materials and labor whose value is not fully recognized, or whose potential as factors of production may not even be recognized at all, into goods and services consumers want and are willing to pay more for than the costs incurred in their production. If the entrepreneurs' returns from consumers exceed their costs, they earn profits. And in the process, they alleviate economic maladjustments. There is nothing normal or guaranteed about profits. An entrepreneur whose ideas, decisions, and actions fail to serve consumers suffers loss.

In the opening essay of this collection, Mises points out the futility of trying to change the world by government planning. His constant themes are that ideas are important, that ideas can change, and that new ideas can change the world. Anyone aware of world events since these articles were written will recognize that new ideas since then have changed the world in many respects, although not always in the freedom direction. How then does Mises recommend planning for freedom? "There is no other planning for freedom and general welfare than to let the market system work."

Bettina Bien Greaves
September 2006

The Free Market Economy versus Government Planning

There is no other planning for freedom and general welfare than to let the market system work.

— "Planning for Freedom"

The alternative is not plan or no plan. The question is: whose planning? Should each member of society plan for himself or should the paternal government alone plan for all?

— "Laissez Faire or Dictatorship"

1

Planning for Freedom

"Planning" and Interventionism

The term 'planning' is mostly used as a synonym for socialism, communism, and authoritarian and totalitarian economic management. Sometimes only the German pattern of socialism—*Zwangswirtschaft**—is called planning, while the term socialism proper is reserved for the Russian pattern of outright socialization and bureaucratic operation of all plants, shops, and farms. At any rate, planning in this sense means all-around planning by the government and enforcement of these plans by the police power. Planning in this sense means full government control of business. It is the antithesis of free enterprise, private initiative, private ownership of the means of production, market economy, and the price system. Planning and capitalism are utterly incompatible. Within a system of planning production is conducted according to the government's orders, not according to the plans of capitalists and entrepreneurs eager to profit by best filling the wants of the consumers.

But the term planning is also used in a second sense. Lord Keynes, Sir William Beveridge, Professor Hansen, and many other eminent men assert that they do not want to substitute totalitarian slavery for freedom. They declare that they are planning for a free society. They recommend a third system, which, as they say, is as far from socialism as it is from capitalism, which, as a third solution of the problem of society's economic organization, stands midway between the two other systems, and while retaining the advantages of both, avoids the disadvantages inherent in each.

Address delivered before the American Academy of Political and Social Science, Philadelphia, Pa., March 30, 1945.
* [Editor's note: "Zwang (German), compulsion; Wirtschaft (German), economy; hence, "compulsory economy."]

These self-styled progressives are certainly mistaken when they pretend that their proposals are new and unheard of. The idea of this third solution is very old indeed, and the French have long since baptized it with a pertinent name; they call it interventionism. Hardly anybody can doubt that history will link the idea of social security, more closely than with the American New Deal and with Sir William Beveridge, with the memory of Bismarck whom our fathers did not precisely describe as a liberal. All the essential ideas of present-day interventionist progressivism were neatly expounded by the supreme brain-trusters of imperial Germany, Professors Schmoller and Wagner, who at the same time urged their Kaiser to invade and to conquer the Americas. Far be it from me to condemn any idea only on account of its not being new. But as the progressives slander all their opponents as old-fashioned, orthodox, and reactionary, it is expedient to observe that it would be more appropriate to speak of the clash of two orthodoxies; the Bismarck orthodoxy versus the Jefferson orthodoxy.

Interventionism

Before entering into an investigation of the interventionist system of a mixed economy two points must be clarified:

First: If within a society based on private ownership of the means of production some of these means are owned and operated by the government or by municipalities, this still does not make for a mixed system which would combine socialism and private ownership. As long as only certain individual enterprises are publicly controlled, the characteristics of the market economy determining economic activity remain essentially unimpaired. The publicly owned enterprises, too, as buyers of raw materials, semi-finished goods, and labor and as sellers of goods and services must fit into the mechanism of the market economy. They are subject to the law of the market; they have to strive after profits or, at least, to avoid losses. When it is attempted to mitigate or to eliminate this dependence by covering the losses of such enterprises with subsidies out of public funds, the only result is a shifting of this dependence somewhere else. This is because the means for the subsidies have to be raised somewhere. They may be raised by collecting taxes. But the burden of such taxes has its effects on the public, not on the government collecting the tax. It is the market, and not the revenue department, which decides upon whom the tax falls and how it affects production and consumption. The market and its inescapable law are supreme.

Second: There are two different patterns for the realization of socialism. The one pattern—we may call it the Marxian or Russian pattern—is purely bureaucratic. All economic enterprises are departments of the government just as the administration of the army and the navy or the postal system. Every single plant, shop, or farm, stands in the same relation to the superior central organization as does a post office to the office of the postmaster general. The whole nation forms one single labor army with compulsory service; the commander of this army is the chief of state.

The second pattern—we may call it the German or *Zwangswirtschaft* system—differs from the first one in that it, seemingly and nominally, maintains private ownership of the means of production, entrepreneurship, and market exchange. So-called entrepreneurs do the buying and selling, pay the workers, contract debts, and pay interest and amortization. But they are no longer entrepreneurs. In Nazi Germany they were called shop managers or *Betriebsführer*. The government tells these seeming entrepreneurs what and how to produce, at what prices and from whom to buy, at what prices and to whom to sell. The government decrees at what wages laborers should work and to whom and under what terms the capitalists should entrust their funds. Market exchange is but a sham. As all prices, wages, and interest rates are fixed by the authority, they are prices, wages, and interest rates in appearance only; in fact they are merely quantitative terms in the authoritarian orders determining each citizen's income, consumption, and standard of living. The authority, not the consumers, directs production. The central board of production management is supreme; all citizens are nothing but civil servants. This is socialism, with the outward appearance of capitalism. Some labels of the capitalistic market economy are retained, but they signify here something entirely different from what they mean in the market economy.

It is necessary to point out this fact to prevent a confusion of socialism and interventionism. The system of hampered market economy or interventionism differs from socialism by the very fact that it is still market economy. The authority seeks to influence the market by the intervention of its coercive power, but it does not want to eliminate the market altogether. It desires that production and consumption should develop along lines different from those prescribed by the unhindered market, and it wants to achieve its aim by injecting into the working of the market orders, commands, and prohibitions for whose enforcement the police power and its apparatus of coercion and compulsion stand ready. But these are isolated interventions; their authors assert that they do not plan to combine these measures into a completely integrated system which regulates all prices, wages, and interest rates, and which thus places full control of production and consumption in the hands of the authorities.

How to Raise Wages

The fundamental principle of those truly liberal economists who are nowadays generally abused as orthodox, reactionaries, and economic royalists is this: There are no means by which the general standard of living can be raised other than by accelerating the increase of capital as compared with population. All that good government can do to improve the material well-being of the masses is to establish and to preserve an institutional setting in which there are no obstacles to the progressive accumulation of new capital and its utilization for the improvement of technical methods of production. The only means to increase a nation's welfare is to increase and to improve the output of products. The only means to raise wage rates permanently for all those eager to earn wages is to raise the productivity of labor by increasing the per-head quota of capital invested and improving the methods of production. Hence, the liberals conclude that the economic policy best fitted to serve the interests of all strata of a nation is free trade both in domestic business and in international relations.

The interventionists, on the contrary, believe that government has the power to improve the masses' standard of living partly at the expense of the capitalists and entrepreneurs, partly at no expense at all. They recommend the restriction of profits and the equalization of incomes and fortunes by confiscatory taxation, the lowering of the rate of interest by an easy money policy and credit expansion, and the raising of the workers' standard of living by the enforcement of minimum wage rates. They advocate lavish government spending. They are, curiously enough, at the same time in favor of low prices for consumers' goods and of high prices for agricultural products.

The liberal economists, that is, those disparaged as orthodox, do not deny that some of these measures can, in the short run, improve the lot of some groups of the population. But, they say, in the long run they must produce effects which, from the point of view of the government and the supporters of its policies, are less desirable than the previous state of affairs they wanted to alter. These measures are, therefore, when judged from the point of view of their own advocates, contrary to purpose.

Depression, the Aftermath of Credit Expansion

It is true, many people believe that economic policy should not bother at all about long-run consequences. They quote a dictum of Lord Keynes: "In the long run we are all dead." I do not question the truth of this statement; I even consider it as the only correct declaration of the neo-British Cambridge school. But the conclusions drawn from this truism are entirely fallacious. The exact diagnosis of the economic evils of our age is: we have outlived the short-run and are suffering from the long-run consequences of policies which did not take them into consideration. The interventionists have silenced the warning voices of the economists. But things developed precisely as these much abused orthodox scholars had predicted. Depression is the aftermath of credit expansion; mass unemployment prolonged year after year is the inextricable effect of attempts to keep wage rates above the level which the unhampered market would have fixed. All those evils which the progressives interpret as evidence of the failure of capitalism are the necessary outcome of allegedly social interference with the market. It is true that many authors who advocated these measures and many statesmen and politicians who executed them were impelled by good intentions and wanted to make people more prosperous. But the means chosen for the attainment of the ends aimed at were inappropriate. However good intentions may be, they can never render unsuitable means any more suitable.

It must be emphasized that we are discussing means and measures, not ends. The matter at issue is not whether the policies advocated by the self-styled progressives are to be recommended or condemned from any arbitrary preconceived point of view. The essential problem is whether such policies can really attain the ends aimed at.

It is beside the mark to confuse the debate by referring to accidental and irrelevant matters. It is useless to divert attention from the main problem by vilifying capitalists and entrepreneurs and by glorifying the virtues of the common man. Precisely because the common man is worthy of all consideration, it is necessary to avoid policies detrimental to his welfare.

The market economy is an integrated system of intertwined factors that mutually condition and determine one another. The social apparatus of coercion and compulsion, i.e., the state, certainly has the might to interfere with the market. The government or agencies in which the government, either by legal privilege or by indulgence, has vested the power to apply violent pressure with impunity are in a position to decree that certain market phenomena are illegal. But such measures do not bring about the results which the interfering power wants to attain. They not only render conditions more unsatisfactory for the interfering authority. They disintegrate the market system altogether, they paralyze its operation, they bring about chaos.

If one considers the working of the market system as unsatisfactory, one must try to substitute another system for it. This is what the socialists aim at. But socialism is not the subject matter of this meeting's discussion. I was invited to deal with interventionism, i.e., with various measures designed to improve the operation of the market system, not to abolish it altogether. And what I contend is that such measures must needs bring about results which from the point of view of their supporters are more undesirable than the previous state of affairs they wanted to alter.

Karl Marx on Labor

Karl Marx did not believe that government or trade union interference with the market can attain the beneficial ends expected. Marx and his consistent followers condemned all such measures in their frank language as reformist nonsense, capitalist fraud, and petty-bourgeois idiocy. They called the supporters of such measures reactionaries. Clemenceau was right when he said: "One is always a reactionary in somebody's opinion."

Karl Marx declared that under capitalism all material goods and likewise labor are commodities, and that socialism will abolish the commodity character both of material goods and of labor. The notion "commodity character" is peculiar to the Marxian doctrine; it was not used before. Its meaning is that goods and labor are negotiated on markets, are sold and bought on the basis of their value. According to Marx the commodity character of labor is implied in the very existence of the wages system. It can disappear only at the "higher stage" of communism as a consequence of the disappearance of the wages system and of payment of wage rates. Marx would have ridiculed the endeavors to abolish the commodity character of labor by an international treaty and the establishment of an International Labor Office and by national legislation and the allocation of money to various national bureaus. I mention these things only in order to show that the progressives are utterly mistaken in referring to Marx and the doctrine of the commodity character of labor in their fight against the economists whom they call reactionary.

Wage Rates and Unemployment

What these old orthodox economists said was this: A permanent rise in wage rates for all people eager to earn wages is only possible as far as the per-head quota of capital invested and concomitantly the productivity of labor increases. It does not benefit the people if minimum wage rates are fixed at a level above that which the unhampered market would have fixed. It does not matter whether this tampering with wage rates is done by government decree or by labor union pressure and compulsion. In either case, the outcome is pernicious to the welfare of a great section of the population.

On an unhampered labor market wage rates are fixed, by the interplay of demand and supply, at a level at which all those eager to work can finally find jobs. On a free labor market unemployment is temporary only and never affects more than a small fraction of the people. There prevails a continuous tendency for unemployment to disappear. But if wage rates are raised by the interference of government or unions above this level, things change. As long as only one part of labor is unionized, the wage rise enforced by the unions does not lead to unemployment, but to an increased supply of labor in those branches of business where there are no efficient unions or no unions at all. The workers who lost their jobs as a consequence of union policy enter the market of the free branches and cause wages to drop in these branches. The corollary of the rise in wages for organized workers is a drop in wages for unorganized workers. But if fixing of wage rates above the potential market level becomes general, workers losing their jobs cannot find employment in other branches. They remain unemployed. Unemployment emerges as a mass phenomenon prolonged year after year.

Such were the teachings of these orthodox economists. Nobody succeeded in refuting them. It was much easier to abuse their authors. Hundreds of treatises, monographs, and pamphlets sneered at them and called them names. Novelists, playwrights, politicians joined the chorus. But truth has its own way. It works and produces effects even if party programs and textbooks refuse to acknowledge it as truth. Events have proved the correctness of the predictions of the orthodox economists. The world faces the tremendous problem of mass unemployment.

It is vain to talk about employment and unemployment without precise reference to a definite rate of wages. The inherent tendency of capitalist evolution is to raise real wage rates steadily. This outcome is the effect of the progressive accumulation of capital by means of which technological methods of production are improved. Whenever the accumulation of additional capital stops, this tendency comes to a standstill. If capital consumption is substituted for an increase of capital available, real wage rates must drop temporarily until the checks to a further increase in capital are removed. The malinvestment, i.e., the squandering of capital that is the most characteristic feature of credit expansion and the orgy of the fictitious boom it produces, the confiscation of profits and fortunes, wars and revolutions are such checks. It is a sad fact that they temporarily lower the masses' standard of living. But these sad facts cannot be brushed away by wishful thinking. There are no other means to remove them than those recommended by the orthodox economists: a sound money policy, thrift in public expenditures, international cooperation for safeguarding durable peace, economic freedom.

The remedies suggested by the unorthodox doctrinaires are futile. Their application makes things worse, not better.

There are well-intentioned men who exhort union leaders to make only moderate use of their powers. But these exhortations are in vain because their authors do not realize that the evils they want to avoid are not due to lack of moderation in the wage policies of the unions. They are the necessary outcome of the whole economic philosophy underlying union activities with regard to wage rates. It is not my task to inquire what good effects unions could possibly bring about in other fields, for instance in education, professional training, and so on. I deal only with their wage policies. The essence of these policies is to prevent the unemployed from finding jobs by underbidding union rates. This policy splits the whole potential labor force into two classes: the employed who earn wages higher than those they would have earned on an unhampered labor market, and the unemployed who do not earn anything at all. In the early thirties money wage rates in this country dropped less than the cost of living. Hourly real wage rates increased in the midst of a catastrophic spread of unemployment. For many of those employed the depression meant a rise in the standard of living, while the unemployed were victimized. The repetition of such conditions can only be avoided by entirely discarding the idea that union compulsion and coercion can benefit all those eager to work and to earn wages. What is needed is not lame warnings. One must convince the workers that the traditional union policies do not serve the interests of all, but only those of one group. While in individual bargaining the unemployed virtually have a voice, they are excluded in collective bargaining. The union officers do not care about the fate of non-members and especially not about that of beginners eager to enter their industry.

Union rates are fixed at a level at which a considerable part of available manpower remains unemployed. Mass unemployment is not proof of the failure of capitalism, but the proof of the failure of traditional union methods.

The same considerations apply to the determination of wage rates by government agencies or by arbitration. If the decision of the government or the arbitrator fixes wage rates at the market level, it is superfluous. If it fixes wage rates at a higher level, it produces mass unemployment.

The fashionable panacea suggested, lavish public spending, is no less futile. If the government provides the funds required by taxing the citizens or by borrowing from the public, it abolishes on the one hand as many jobs as it creates on the other. If government spending is financed by borrowing from commercial banks, it means credit expansion and inflation. Then the prices of all commodities and services must rise, whatever the government does to prevent this outcome.

If in the course of an inflation the rise in commodity prices exceeds the rise in nominal wage rates, unemployment will drop. But what makes unemployment shrink is precisely the fact that real wage rates are falling. Lord Keynes recommended credit expansion because he believed that the wage earners will acquiesce in this outcome; he believed that "a gradual and automatic lowering of real wage rates as a result of rising prices" would not be so strongly resisted by labor as an attempt to lower money wage rates. It is very unlikely that this will happen. Public opinion is fully aware of the changes in purchasing power and watches with burning interest the movements of the index of commodity prices and of cost of living. The substance of all discussions concerning wage rates is real wage rates, not nominal wage rates. There is no prospect of outsmarting the unions by such tricks.

But even if Lord Keynes's assumption were correct, no good could come from such a deception. Great conflicts of ideas must be solved by straight and frank methods; they cannot be solved by artifices and make-shifts. What is needed is not to throw dust into the eyes of the workers, but to convince them. They themselves must realize that the traditional union methods do not serve their interests. They themselves must abandon of their own accord policies that harm both them and all other people.

The Role of Profit and Loss

What those allegedly planning for freedom do not comprehend is that the market with its prices is the steering mechanism of the free enterprise system. Flexibility of commodity prices, wage rates and interest rates is instrumental in adapting production to the changing conditions and needs of the consumers and in discarding backward technological methods. If these adjustments are not brought about by the interplay of the forces operating on the market, they must be enforced by government orders. This means full government control, the Nazi *Zwangswirtschaft*. There is no middle way. The attempts to keep commodity prices rigid, to raise wage rates and to lower interest rates ad libitum only paralyze the system. They create a state of affairs which does not satisfy anybody. They must be either abandoned by a return to freedom of the market, or they must be completed by pure and undisguised socialism.

The inequality of income and fortunes is essential in capitalism. The progressives consider profits as objectionable. The very existence of profits is in their eyes a proof that wage rates could be raised without harm to anybody else than idle parasites. They speak of profit without dealing with its corollary, loss. Profit and loss are the instruments by means of which the consumers keep a tight rein on all entrepreneurial activities. A profitable enterprise tends to expand, an unprofitable one tends to shrink. The elimination of profit renders production rigid and abolishes the consumers' sovereignty. This will happen not because the enterprisers are mean and greedy, and lack these monkish virtues of self-sacrifice which the planners ascribe to all other people. In the absence of profits the entrepreneurs would not learn what the wants of the consumers are, and if they were to guess, they would not have the means to adjust and to expand their plants accordingly. Profits and losses withdraw the material factors of production from the hands of the inefficient and convey them into the hands of the more efficient. It is their social function to make a man the more influential in the conduct of business the better he succeeds in producing commodities for which people scramble.

It is therefore beyond the point to apply to profits the yardstick of personal merit or happiness. Of course, Mr. X would probably be as happy with 10 millions as with 100 millions. From a metaphysical point of view, it is certainly inexplicable why Mr. X should make 2 millions a year, while the chief justice or the nation's foremost philosophers and poets make much less. But the question is not about Mr. X; it is about the consumers. Would the consumers be better and more cheaply supplied if the law were to prevent the most efficient entrepreneurs from expanding the sphere of their activities? The answer is clearly in the negative. If the present tax rates had been in effect from the beginning of our century, many who are millionaires today would live under more modest circumstances. But all those new branches of industry which supply the masses with articles unheard of before would operate, if at all, on a much smaller scale, and their products would be beyond the reach of the common man.

The Market System Serves the Common Man

The market system makes all men in their capacity as producers responsible to the consumer. This dependence is direct with entrepreneurs, capitalists, farmers, and professional men, and indirect with people working for salaries and wages. The economic system of the division of labor, in which everybody provides for his own needs by serving other people, cannot operate if there is no factor adjusting the producers' efforts to the wishes of those for whom they produce. If the market is not allowed to steer the whole economic apparatus, the government must do it.

The socialist plans are absolutely wrong and unrealizable. This is another subject. But the socialist writers are at least clear-sighted enough to see that simply to paralyze the market system results in nothing but chaos. When they favor such acts of sabotage and destruction, they do so because they believe that the chaos brought about will pave the way for socialism. But those who pretend that they want to preserve freedom, while they are eager to fix prices, wage rates, and interest rates at a level different from that of the market, delude themselves. There is no other alternative to totalitarian slavery than liberty. There is no other planning for freedom and general welfare than to let the market system work. There is no other means to attain full employment, rising real wage rates, and a high standard of living for the common man than private initiative and free enterprise.

2

Laissez Faire or Dictatorship

What the "Encyclopaedia of the Social Sciences" Says about Laissez Faire

For more than a hundred years the maxim *laissez faire, laissez passer* has been a red rag to harbingers of totalitarian despotism. As these zealots see it, this maxim condenses all the shameful principles of capitalism. To unmask its fallacies is therefore tantamount to exploding the ideological foundations of the system of private ownership of the means of production, and implicitly demonstrating the excellence of its antithesis, viz., communism and socialism.

The *Encyclopaedia of the Social Sciences* may fairly be considered as representative of the doctrines taught at American and British universities and colleges. Its ninth volume contains an article "Laissez Faire" from the pen of the Oxford professor and author of detective stories, G. D. H. Cole. In the five and a quarter pages of his contribution Professor Cole freely indulges in the use of deprecatory epithets. The maxim "cannot stand examination," it is only prevalent in "popular economics," it is "theoretically bankrupt," an "anachronism," it survives only as a "prejudice," but "as a doctrine deserving of theoretical respect it is dead." Resort to these and many other similar opprobrious appellations fails to disguise the fact that Professor Cole's arguments entirely miss the point. Professor Cole is not qualified to deal with the problems involved because he simply does not know what the market economy is and how it works. The only correct affirmation of his article is the truism that those rejecting laissez faire are Socialists. He is also right in declaring that the refutation of laissez faire is "as prominent in the national idea of Fascism in Italy as in Russian Communism."

Originally published in *Plain Talk*, January 1949. Reprinted with permission from the Foundation for Economic Education.

The volume which contains Mr. Cole's article was published in January 1933. This explains why he did not include Nazi Germany in the ranks of those nations which have freed themselves from the spell of the sinister maxim. He merely registers with satisfaction that the conception rejecting laissez faire is "at the back of many projects of national planning which, largely under Russian influence, is now being put forward all over the world."

Laissez Faire Means Free Market Economy

Learned historians have bestowed much pains upon the question to whom the origin of the maxim *laissez faire, laissez passer* is to be attributed.* At any rate it is certain that in the second part of the eighteenth century the outstanding French champions of economic freedom—foremost among them Gournay, Quesnay, Turgot, and Mirabeau—compressed their program for popular use into this sentence. Their aim was the establishment of the unhampered market economy. In order to attain this end they advocated the abolition of all statutes preventing the more industrious and more efficient people from outdoing the less industrious and less efficient competitors and restricting the mobility of commodities and of men. It was this that the famous maxim was designed to express.

In occasionally using the words *laissez faire, laissez passer*, the eighteenth century economists did not intend to baptize their social philosophy the laissez-faire doctrine. They concentrated their efforts upon the elaboration of a new system of social and political ideas which would benefit mankind. They were not eager to organize a faction or party and to find a name for it. It was only later, in the second decade of the nineteenth century, that a term came to signify the total complex of the political philosophy of freedom, viz., liberalism. The new word was borrowed from Spain where it designated the friends of constitutional government and religious freedom. Very soon it was used all over Europe as a label for the endeavors of those who stood for representative government, freedom of thought, of speech and of the press, private ownership of the means of production, and free trade.

The liberal program is an indivisible and indissoluble whole, not

---

* Cf. especially A. Oncken, *Die Maxime laissez faire et laissez passer, ihr Ursprung, ihr Werden*, Bern 1886; G. Schelle, *Vincent de Gournay*, Paris 1897, pp. 214–26.

an arbitrarily assembled patchwork of diverse components. Its various parts condition one another. The idea that political freedom can be preserved in the absence of economic freedom, and vice versa, is an illusion. Political freedom is the corollary of economic freedom. It is no accident that the age of capitalism became also the age of government by the people. If individuals are not free to buy and to sell on the market, they turn into virtual slaves dependent on the good graces of the omnipotent government, whatever the wording of the constitution may be.

The fathers of socialism and modern interventionism were fully aware that their own programs were incompatible with the political postulates of liberalism. The main target of their passionate attacks was liberalism as a whole. They did not make a distinction between the political and the economic aspects of liberalism.

But as the years went on, the Socialists and interventionists of the Anglo-Saxon countries discovered that it was a hopeless venture to attack liberalism and the idea of liberty *openly*. The prestige of liberal institutions was so overwhelming in the English-speaking world that no party could risk defying them directly. Anti-liberalism's only chance was to camouflage itself as true and genuine liberalism and to denounce the attitudes of all other parties as a mere counterfeit liberalism.

The continental Socialists had fanatically smeared and disparaged liberalism and progressivism, and contemptuously derogated democracy as "pluto-democracy." Their Anglo-Saxon imitators, who at first had adopted the same procedure, after a while reversed their semantics and arrogated to themselves the appellations liberal, progressive and democratic. They began flatly to deny that political freedom is the corollary of economic freedom. They boldly asserted that democratic institutions can work satisfactorily only where the government has full control of all production activities and the individual citizen is bound to obey unconditionally all orders issued by the central planning board. In their eyes all-round regimentation is the only means to make people free, and freedom of the press is best guaranteed by a government monopoly of printing and publishing. They were not plagued by any scruples when they stole the good old name of liberalism and began to call their own tenets and policies liberal. In this country the term "liberalism" is nowadays more often than not used as a synonym for communism.

The semantic innovation which the Socialists and interventionists thus inaugurated left the advocates of freedom without any name. There was no term available to call those who believe that private ownership of the material factors of production is the best, in fact, the only means to make the nation and all its individual citizens as prosperous as possible and to make representative government work. The Socialists and interventionists believe that such people do not deserve any name, but are to be referred to only by such insulting epithets as "economic royalists," "Wall Street sycophants," "reactionaries," and so on.

This state of affairs explains why the phrase laissez faire was more and more used to signify the ideas of those who advocate the free market economy as against government planning and regimentation.

The Cairnes Argument against Laissez Faire

Today it is no longer difficult for intelligent men to realize that the alternative is market economy or communism. Production can either be directed by buying and abstention from buying on the part of all people, or it can be directed by the orders of the supreme chief of state. Men must choose between these two systems of society's economic organization. There is no third solution, no middle way.

It is a sad fact that not only politicians and demagogues have failed to see this essential truth, but that even some economists have erred in dealing with the problems involved.

There is no need to dwell upon the unfortunate influence which originated from John Stuart Mill's confused treatment of government interference with business. It becomes evident from Mill's *Autobiography* that his change of mind resulting in what he calls "a greater approximation . . . to a qualified socialism" * was motivated by purely personal feelings and affections and not by emotionally undisturbed reasoning. It is certainly one of the tasks of economics to refute the errors which deform the disquisitions of so eminent a thinker as Mill. But it is unnecessary to argue against the prepossessions of Mrs. Mill.

A few years after Mill, another outstanding economist, J. E. Cairnes, dealt with the same problem.† As a philosopher and essayist Mill by far

---

* Cf. John Stuart Mill, *Autobiography*, London 1873, p. 191.
† Cf. J. E. Cairnes, "Political Economy and Laissez Faire," an introductory lecture delivered in University College, London, November, 1870; reprinted in *Essays in Political Economy*, London 1873, pp. 232–64.

supersedes Cairnes. But as an economist Cairnes was not second to Mill, and his contributions to the epistemology of the social sciences are of incomparably greater value and importance than those of Mill. Yet, Cairnes's analysis of laissez faire does not display that brilliant precision of reasoning which is the distinguishing mark of his other writings.

As Cairnes sees it, the assertion implied in the doctrine of laissez faire is that "the promptings of self-interest will lead individuals, in all that range of their conduct which has to do with their material well-being, spontaneously to follow that course which is most for their own good and for the good of all." This assertion, he says, "involves the two following assumptions: first, that the interests of human beings are fundamentally the same—that what is most for my interest is also most for the interest of other people; and, secondly, that individuals know their interests in the sense in which they are coincident with the interests of others, and that, in the absence of coercion, they will in this sense follow them. If these two propositions be made out, the policy of laissez faire . . . follows with scientific rigour."

Cairnes is disposed to accept the first—the major—premise of the syllogism, that the interests of human beings are fundamentally the same. But he rejects the second—the minor—premise.* "Human beings know and follow their interests according to their lights and dispositions; but not necessarily, nor in practice always, in the sense in which the interest of the individual is coincident with that of others and of the whole." †

Let us for the sake of argument accept the way in which Cairnes presents the problem and in which he argues. Human beings are fallible and therefore sometimes fail to learn what their true interests would require them to do. Furthermore, there are "such things in the world as passion, prejudice, custom, *esprit de corps*, class interest, to draw people aside from the pursuit of their interests in the largest and highest sense." ‡ It is very unfortunate that reality is such. But, we must ask, is there any means available to prevent mankind from being hurt by people's bad judgment and malice? Is it not a non sequitur to as-

---

* Cf. Cairnes, l.c., pp. 244–45.
† Cf. Cairnes, l.c., p. 250.
‡ Cf. Cairnes, l.c., p. 246.

sume that one could avoid the disastrous consequences of these human weaknesses by substituting the government's discretion for that of the individual citizens? Are governments endowed with intellectual and moral perfection? Are the rulers not human too, not themselves subject to human frailties and deficiencies?

The theocratic doctrine is consistent in attributing to the head of the government superhuman powers. The French royalists contend that the solemn consecration at Rheims conveys to the king of France, anointed with the sacred oil which a dove from Heaven brought down for the consecration of Clovis, divine dispensation. The legitimate king cannot err and cannot do wrong, and his royal touch miraculously cures scrofula. No less consistent was the late German professor Werner Sombart in declaring that *Führertum* is a permanent revelation and that the *Führer* gets his orders directly from God, the supreme *Führer* of the Universe.* Once you admit these premises, you can no longer raise any objections against planning and socialism. Why tolerate the incompetence of clumsy and ill-intentioned bunglers if you can be made happy and prosperous by the God-sent authority?

But Cairnes is not prepared to accept "the principle of State control, the doctrine of paternal government." † His disquisitions peter out in vague and contradictory talk that leaves the relevant question unanswered. He does not comprehend that it is indispensable to choose between the supremacy of individuals and that of the government. Some agency must determine how the factors of production should be employed and what should be produced. If it is not the consumer, by means of buying and abstention from buying on the market, it must be the government by compulsion.

If one rejects laissez faire on account of man's fallibility and moral weakness, one must for the same reasons also reject every kind of government action. Cairnes's mode of arguing, provided it is not integrated into a theocratic philosophy in the manner of the French royalists or the German Nazis, leads to complete anarchism and nihilism.

One of the distortions to which the self-styled "progressives" resort in smearing laissez faire is the statement that consistent application of laissez faire must result in anarchy. There is no need to dwell upon this

---

* Cf. W. Sombart, *Deutscher Sozialismus*, Charlottenburg 1934, p. 213 (American edition: A *New Social Philosophy*, translated by K. F. Geiser, Princeton 1937, p. 194).
† Cf. Cairnes, l.c., p. 251.

fallacy. It is more important to stress the fact that Cairnes's argument against laissez faire, when consistently carried through to its inevitable logical consequences, is essentially anarchistic.

"Conscious Planning" versus "Automatic Forces"

As the self-styled "progressives" see things, the alternative is: "automatic forces" or "conscious planning." * It is obvious, they go on saying, that to rely upon automatic processes is sheer stupidity. No reasonable man can seriously recommend doing nothing and letting things go without any interference through purposive action. A plan, by the very fact that it is a display of conscious action, is incomparably superior to the absence of any planning. Laissez faire means: let evils last and do not try to improve the lot of mankind by reasonable action.

This is utterly fallacious and deceptive talk. The argument advanced for planning is derived entirely from an inadmissable interpretation of a metaphor. It has no foundation other than the connotations implied in the term "automatic," which is customarily applied in a metaphorical sense to describe the market process. Automatic, says the *Concise Oxford Dictionary*, means "unconscious, unintelligent, merely mechanical." Automatic, says *Webster's Collegiate Dictionary*, means "not subject to the control of the will . . . performed without active thought and without conscious intention or direction." What a triumph for the champion of planning to play this trump-card!

The truth is that the choice is not between a dead mechanism and a rigid automatism on the one hand and conscious planning on the other hand. The alternative is not plan or no plan. The question is: whose planning? Should each member of society plan for himself or should the paternal government alone plan for all? The issue is not *automatism versus conscious action*; it is *spontaneous action of each individual versus the exclusive action of the government*. It is *freedom versus government omnipotence*.

Laissez faire does not mean: let soulless mechanical forces operate. It means: let individuals choose how they want to cooperate in the social division of labor and let them determine what the entrepreneurs

---

* Cf. A. H. Hansen, "Social Planning for Tomorrow," in *The United States after the War*, Cornell University Lectures, Ithaca 1945, pp. 32–33.

should produce. Planning means: let the government alone choose and enforce its rulings by the apparatus of coercion and compulsion.

The Satisfaction of Man's "True" Needs

Under laissez faire, says the planner, the goods produced are not those which people "really" need, but those goods from the sale of which the highest returns are expected. It is the objective of planning to direct production toward the satisfaction of "true" needs. But who should decide what "true" needs are?

Thus, for instance, Professor Harold Laski, the former chairman of the British Labor Party, determined the objective of planned direction of investment as "the use of the investor's savings will be in housing rather than in cinemas." * It does not matter whether or not one agrees with the professor's personal view that better houses are more important than moving pictures. The fact is that consumers, by spending part of their money for admission to the movies, have made another choice. If the masses of Great Britain, the same people whose votes swept the Labor Party into power, were to stop patronizing the moving pictures and to spend more for comfortable homes and apartments, profit-seeking business would be forced to invest more in building homes and apartment houses, and less in the production of swanky pictures. What Professor Laski aimed at is to defy the wishes of the consumers and to substitute his own will for theirs. He wanted to do away with the democracy of the market and to establish the absolute rule of a production czar. He might pretend that he is right from a "higher" point of view, and that as a superman he is called upon to impose his own set of values on the masses of inferior men. But then he should have been frank enough to say so plainly.

All this passionate praise of the super-eminence of government action is merely a poor disguise for the individual interventionist's self-deification. The Great God State is great only because it is expected to do exclusively what the individual advocate of interventionism wants to be achieved. The only true plan is the one of which the individual planner fully approves. All other plans are simply counterfeit. What the author of a book on the benefits of planning has in mind is, of course,

---

* Cf. Laski's broadcast, *Revolution by Consent*, reprinted in *Talks*, Vol. X, Number 10, p. 7 (October 1945).

always his own plan alone. No planner was ever shrewd enough to consider the possibility that the plan which the government will put into practice could differ from his own plan.

The various planners agree only with regard to their rejection of laissez faire, i.e., the individual's discretion to choose and to act. They disagree entirely on the choice of the unique plan to be adopted. To every exposure of the manifest and incontestable defects of interventionist policies the champions of interventionism always react in the same way. These faults, they say, were the sins of spurious interventionism; what *we* are advocating is *good* interventionism. And, of course, good interventionism is the professor's own brand only.

"Positive" Policies versus "Negative" Policies

In dealing with the ascent of modern statism, socialism and interventionism, one must not neglect the preponderant role played by the pressure groups and lobbies of civil servants and those university graduates who longed for government jobs. Two associations were paramount in Europe's progress toward "social reform": the Fabian Society in England and the *Verein für Sozialpolitik* in Germany. The Fabian Society had in its earlier days a "wholly disproportionate representation of civil servants."* With regard to the *Verein für Sozialpolitik*, one of its founders and most eminent leaders, Professor Lujo Brentano, admitted that at the beginning it called for no other response than from the civil servants.†

It is not surprising that the civil service mentality was reflected in the semantic practices of the new factions. Seen from the point of view of the particular group interests of the bureaucrats, every measure that makes the government's payroll swell is progress. Politicians who favor such a measure make a *positive* contribution to welfare, while those who object are *negative*. Very soon this linguistic innovation became general. The interventionists, in claiming for themselves the appellation "liberal," explained that they, of course, were liberals with a positive program as distinguished from the merely negative program of the "orthodox" laissez-faire people.

Thus he who advocates tariffs, censorship, foreign exchange control,

* Cf. A. Gray, *The Socialist Tradition Moses to Lenin*, London 1946, p. 385.
† Cf. L. Brentano, *Ist das "System Brentano" zusammengebrochen?*, Berlin 1918, p. 19.

price control supports a positive program that will provide jobs for customs officers, censors, and employees of the offices for price control and foreign exchange control. But free traders and advocates of the freedom of the press are bad citizens; they are negative. Laissez faire is the embodiment of negativism, while socialism, in converting all people into government employees, is 100 percent positive. The more a former liberal completes his defection from liberalism and approaches socialism, the more "positive" does he become.

It is hardly necessary to stress that this is all nonsense. Whether an idea is enunciated in an affirmative or in a negative proposition depends entirely on the form which the author chooses to give it. The "negative" proposition, *I am against censorship*, is identical with the "positive" proposition, *I am in favor of everybody's right to publicize his opinions*. Laissez faire is not even formally a negative formula; rather it is the contrary of laissez faire that would sound negative. Essentially, the maxim asks for private ownership of the means of production. This implies, of course, that it rejects socialism. The supporters of laissez faire object to government interference with business not because they "hate" the "state" or because they are committed to a "negative" program. They object to it because it is incompatible with their own positive program, the free market economy.*

Conclusion

Laissez faire means: let the individual citizen, the much talked-about common man, choose and act and do not force him to yield to a dictator.

---

* The present writer refuted this distinction between "positive" and "constructive" socialism and interventionism on the one hand, and "negative" liberalism of the laissez-faire type on the other in his article "Sozialliberalismus," first published in 1926 in *Zeitschrift für die Gesamte Staatswissenschaft*, and reprinted in 1929 in his book *Kritik des Interventionismus*, pp. 55–90. [Editor's note: This article was translated as "Social Liberalism" and published in *A Critique of Interventionism* (New Rochelle, N. Y.: Arlington House, 1977), pp. 71–106; 2d revised ed., *Critique of Interventionism* (Irvington-on-Hudson, N. Y.: Foundation for Economic Education, 1996), pp. 43–70.]

3

Capital Supply and American Prosperity

One of the amazing phenomena of the present election campaign is the way in which speakers and writers refer to the state of business and to the economic condition of the nation. They praise the administration for the prosperity and for the high standard of living of the average citizen. "You never had it so good," they say, and, "Don't let them take it away." It is implied that the increase in the quantity and the improvement in the quality of products available for consumption are achievements of a paternal government. The incomes of the individual citizens are viewed as handouts graciously bestowed upon them by a benevolent bureaucracy. The American government is considered as better than that of Italy or of India because it passes into the hands of the citizens more and better products than they do.

Capital Investment Increases Production

It is hardly possible to misrepresent in a more thorough way the fundamental facts of economics. The average standard of living is in this country higher than in any other country of the world, not because the American statesmen and politicians are superior to the foreign statesmen and politicians, but because the per-head quota of capital invested is in America higher than in other countries. Average output per man-hour is in this country higher than in other countries, whether England or India, because the American plants are equipped with more efficient tools and machines. Capital is more plentiful in America than it is in other countries because up to now the institutions and laws of the United States put fewer obstacles in the way of big-scale capital accumulation than did those foreign countries.

Address delivered before the University Club of Milwaukee (Wisconsin) on October 13, 1952.

It is not true that the economic backwardness of foreign countries is to be imputed to technological ignorance on the part of their peoples. Modern technology is by and large no esoteric doctrine. It is taught at many technological universities in this country as well as abroad. It is described in many excellent textbooks and articles of scientific magazines. Hundreds of aliens are every year graduated from American technological institutes. There are in every part of the earth many experts perfectly conversant with the most recent developments of industrial technique. It is not a lack of the "know-how" that prevents foreign countries from fully adopting American methods of manufacturing, but the insufficiency of capital available.

Under Capitalism, Individual Responsibility and Thrift Are Appreciated

The climate of opinion in which capitalism could thrive was characterized by the moral approbation of the individual citizen's eagerness to provide for his own and his family's future. Thrift was appreciated as a virtue no less beneficial to the individual saver himself than to all other people. If people do not consume their whole incomes, the non-consumed surplus can be invested, it increases the amount of capital goods available and thereby makes it possible to embark upon projects which could not be executed before. Progressive capital accumulation results in perpetual economic betterment. All aspects of every citizen's life are favorably affected. The continuous tendency toward an expansion of business activities opens an ample field for the display of the energies of the rising generation. Looking backward upon his youth and the conditions in his parent's home, the average man cannot help realizing that there is progress toward a more satisfactory standard of living.

Such were the conditions in all countries on the eve of the First World War. Conditions were certainly not everywhere the same. There were the countries of Western Capitalism on the one hand, and on the other hand the backward nations which were slow and reluctant in adopting the ideas and the methods of modern progressive business. But these backward nations were amply benefited by the investment of capital provided by the capitalists of the advanced nations. Foreign capital built their railroads and factories and developed their natural resources.

The spectacle that the world offers today is very different. As it was forty years ago, the world is divided into two camps. There is, on the one hand, the capitalist orbit, considerably shrunk when compared with its size in 1914. It includes today the United States and Canada and some of the small nations of Western Europe. The much greater part of the earth's population lives in countries strictly rejecting the methods of private property, initiative, and enterprise. These countries are either stagnating or faced with a progressive deterioration of their economic conditions.

United States Living Standards

Let us illustrate this difference by contrasting, as typical of each of the two groups, conditions in this country and those in India.

In the United States, capitalist big business almost every year supplies the masses with some novelties: either improved articles to replace similar articles used long since or things which had been altogether unknown before. The latter—as for instance, television sets or nylon hosiery—are commonly called luxuries, as people previously lived rather contented and happy without them. The average common man enjoys a standard of living which, only fifty years ago, his parents or grandparents would have considered as fabulous. His home is equipped with gadgets and facilities which the well-to-do of earlier ages would have envied. His wife and his daughters dress elegantly and apply cosmetics. His children, well fed and cared for, have the benefit of a high school education, many also of a college education. If one observes him and his family on their weekend outings, one must admit that he looks prosperous.

There are, of course, also Americans whose material conditions appear unsatisfactory when compared with those of the great majority of the nation. Some authors of novels and plays would have us believe that their gloomy descriptions of the lot of this unfortunate minority is representative of the fate of the common man under capitalism. They are mistaken. The plight of these wretched Americans is rather representative of conditions as they prevailed everywhere in the precapitalistic ages and still prevail in the countries which were either not at all or only superficially touched by capitalism. What is wrong with these people is that they have not yet been integrated into the frame of capitalist production. Their penury is a remnant of the past. The progressive accumulation of new capital and the expansion of big-scale production will eradicate it by the same methods by means of which it has already improved the standard of living of the immense majority, viz., by raising the per-head quota of capital invested and thereby the marginal productivity of labor.

India's Living Standards

Now let us look at India. Nature has endowed its territory with valuable resources, perhaps more richly than the soil of the United States. On the other hand, climatic conditions make it possible for man to subsist on a lighter diet and to do without many things which in the rough winter of the greater part of the United States are indispensable. Nonetheless, the masses of India are on the verge of starvation, shabbily dressed, crammed into primitive huts, dirty, illiterate. From year to year things are getting worse; for population figures are increasing while the total amount of capital invested does not increase or, even more likely, decreases. At any rate, there is a progressive drop in the per-head quota of capital invested.

Laissez Faire Ideas Brought Industrialization to England

In the middle of the eighteenth century conditions in England were hardly more propitious than they are today in India. The traditional system of production was not fit to provide for the needs of an increasing population. The number of people for whom there was no room left in the rigid system of paternalism and government tutelage of business grew rapidly. Although at that time England's population was not much more than fifteen percent of what it is today, there were several millions of destitute poor. Neither the ruling aristocracy nor these paupers themselves had any idea about what could be done to improve the material conditions of the masses.

The great change that within a few decades made England the world's wealthiest and most powerful nation was prepared for by a small group of philosophers and economists. They demolished entirely the pseudo-philosophy that hitherto had been instrumental in shaping the economic policies of the nations. They exploded the old fables: (1) that it is unfair and unjust to outdo a competitor by producing better and cheaper goods; (2) that it is iniquitous to deviate from traditional methods of production; (3) that labor-saving machines bring about unemployment and are therefore an evil; (4) that it is one of the tasks of civil government to prevent efficient businessmen from getting rich and to protect the less efficient against the competition of the more efficient; and (5) that to restrict the freedom and the initiative of entrepreneurs by government compulsion or by coercion on the part of other powers is an appropriate means to promote a nation's well-being. In short: these authors expounded the doctrine of free trade and laissez faire. They paved the way for a policy that no longer obstructed the businessman's effort to improve and to expand his operations.

What begot modern industrialization and the unprecedented improvement in material conditions that it brought about was neither capital previously accumulated nor previously assembled technological knowledge. In England, as well as in the other Western countries that followed it on the path of capitalism, the early pioneers of capitalism started with scanty capital and scanty technological experience. At the outset of industrialization was the philosophy of private enterprise and initiative, and the practical application of this ideology made the capital swell and the technological know-how advance and ripen.

One must stress this point because its neglect misleads the statesmen of all backward nations in their plans for economic improvement. They think that industrialization means machines and textbooks of technology. In fact, it means economic freedom that creates both capital and technological knowledge.

India Lacks Capitalist Ideas

Let us look again at India. India lacks capital because it never adopted the pro-capitalist philosophy of the West and therefore did not remove the traditional institutional obstacles to free enterprise and big-scale accumulation. Capitalism came to India as an alien imported ideology that never took root in the minds of the people. Foreign, mostly British, capital built railroads and factories. The natives looked askance not only upon the activities of the alien capitalists but no less upon those of their countrymen who cooperated in the capitalist ventures. Today the situation is this: Thanks to new methods of therapeutics, developed by the capitalist nations and imported to India by the British, the average length of life has been prolonged and the population is rapidly increasing. As the foreign capitalists have either already been virtually expropriated or have to face expropriation in the near future, there can no longer be any question of new investment of foreign capital.

On the other hand, the accumulation of domestic capital is prevented by the manifest hostility of the government apparatus and the ruling party.

The Indian government talks a lot about industrialization. But what it really has in mind is nationalization of already existing privately owned industries. For the sake of argument, we may neglect referring to the fact that this will probably result in a progressive decumulation of the capital invested in these industries as was the case in most of the countries that have experimented with nationalization. At any rate, nationalization as such does not add anything to the already prevailing extent of investment. Mr. Nehru admits that his government does not have the capital required for the establishment of new state-owned industries or for the expansion of such industries already existing. Thus, he solemnly declares that his government will give to private industries "encouragement in every way." And he explains in what this encouragement will consist: we will promise them, he says, "that we would not touch them for at least ten years, maybe more." He adds: "We do not know when we shall nationalize them."* But the businessmen know very well that new investments will be nationalized as soon as they begin to yield returns.

Envy Fosters Anti-capitalism

I have dwelt so long upon the affairs of India because they are representative of what is going on today almost in all parts of Asia and Africa, in great parts of Latin America and even in many European countries. In all these countries the population is increasing. In all these countries foreign investments are expropriated, either openly or surreptitiously by means of foreign exchange control or discriminatory taxation. At the same time, their domestic policies do their best to discourage the formation of domestic capital. There is much poverty in the world today; and the governments, in this regard in full agreement with public opinion, perpetuate and aggravate this poverty by their policies.

As these people see it, their economic troubles were in some unspecified way caused by the capitalist countries of the West. This notion included, until a few years ago, also the advanced nations of West-

---

* Cf. Jawaharlal Nehru, *Independence and After: A Collection of Speeches, 1946–1949*, New York 1950, page 192.

ern Europe, especially also the United Kingdom. With recent economic changes, the number of nations to which it refers has been more and more restricted; today it means practically only the United States. The inhabitants of all those countries in which the average income is considerably lower than in this country look upon the United States with the same feelings of envy and hatred with which within the capitalist countries those voting the ticket of the various communist, socialist and interventionist parties look upon the entrepreneurs of their own nation. The same slogans that are employed in our domestic antagonisms—such as Wall Street, big business, monopolies, merchants of death—are resorted to in speeches and articles by the anti-American politicians when they are attacking what is called in Latin America, Yankeeism, and in the other hemisphere, Americanism. In these effusions there is little difference between the most chauvinistic nationalists and the most enthusiastic adepts of Marxian internationalism, between the self-styled conservatives eager to preserve traditional religious faith and political institutions, and the revolutionaries aiming at the violent overthrow of all that exists.

The popularity of these ideas is by no means an effect of the inflammatory propaganda of the Soviets. It is just the other way round. The communist lies and calumnies get their persuasiveness, whatever it may be, from the fact that they agree with the socio-political doctrines taught at most of the universities and held by the most influential politicians and writers.

Anti-capitalistic Ideas Are Worldwide

The same ideas dominate the minds in this country and determine the attitude of statesmen with regard to all the problems concerned. People are ashamed of the fact that American capital developed the natural resources in many countries which lacked both the capital and the trained specialists required. When various foreign governments expropriated American investments or repudiated loans granted by the American saver, the public either remained indifferent or even sympathized with the expropriators. With the ideas underlying the programs of the most influential political groups and taught at most of the educational institutions, no other reaction could be expected.

Four years ago there assembled in Amsterdam the World Council of Churches, an organization of one-hundred-and-fifty-odd denominations. We read in the report drafted by this ecumenical body the follow-ing statement: "Justice demands that the inhabitants of Asia and Africa should have the benefits of more machine production." This implies that the technological backwardness of these nations has been caused by an injustice committed by some individuals, groups of individuals or nations. The culprits are not specified. But it is understood that the indictment refers to the capitalists and businessmen of the shrinking number of capitalist countries, practically to the United States and Canada. Such is the opinion of very judicious conservative churchmen acting in full awareness of their responsibilities.

The same doctrine is at the bottom of the foreign aid and the Point Four policies of the United States. It is implied that the American tax-payers have the moral obligation to provide capital for nations that have expropriated foreign investments and are preventing the accumulation of domestic capital by various schemes.

There is no use indulging in wishful thinking. Under the present state of international law foreign investments are unsafe and at the mercy of each sovereign nation's government. It is generally agreed that every sovereign government has the right to decree a fictitious parity of its inflated currency as against dollars or gold and to try to enforce this arbitrarily fixed spurious parity by foreign exchange control, that is, by virtually expropriating foreign investors. As far as some foreign govern-ments still abstain from such confiscations, they do so because they hope to talk foreigners into more investments and thus to be later in a position to expropriate more.

In the ranks of those nations that do all that can be done to prevent their industries from getting badly needed capital, we find today also Great Britain, once the cradle of free enterprise and before 1914 the world's richest or second richest country. In exuberant and entirely un-deserved praise of the late Lord Keynes, a Harvard professor found in his hero but one weakness. Keynes, he said, "always exalted what was at any moment truth and wisdom for England into truth and wisdom for all times and places." * I heartily disagree. Just at the moment in which it must have become manifest to every judicious observer that England's economic distress was caused by an insufficient supply of capital, Keynes enounced his notorious doctrine of the alleged dangers

* Cf. J. Schumpeter, "Keynes, the Economist," in *The New Economics*, ed. by S. E. Harris, New York 1947, page 85.

of saving and passionately recommended more spending. Keynes tried to provide a belated and spurious justification of a policy that Great Britain had adopted in defiance of the teachings of all its great economists. The essence of Keynesianism is its complete failure to conceive the role that saving and capital accumulation play in the improvement of economic conditions.

Importance of Capital Savings

The main problem for this country is: Will the United States follow the course of the economic policies adopted by almost all foreign nations, even by many of those which had been foremost in the evolution of capitalism? Up to now in this country the amount of savings and formation of new capital still exceeds the amount of dissaving and decumulation of capital. Will this last?

To answer such a question one must look upon the ideas about economic matters held by public opinion. The question is: Do the American voters know that the unprecedented improvement in their standard of living that the last hundred years brought was the result of the steady rise in the per-head quota of capital invested? Do they realize that every measure leading to capital decumulation jeopardizes their prosperity? Are they aware of the conditions that make their wage rates tower above those of other countries?

If we pass in review the speeches of political leaders, the editorials of newspapers and textbooks of economics and finance, we cannot help discovering that very little attention, if at all, is paid to the problems of capital equipment. Most people take it simply for granted that some mysterious factor is operative that makes the nation richer from year to year. Government economists have computed a rate of yearly increase in the national income for the past fifty years and blithely assume that in the future the same rate will prevail. They discuss problems of taxation without even mentioning the fact that our present tax system collects large funds, which would have been saved by the taxpayer, and employs them for current expenditure.

A typical instance of this mode of dealing (or rather, nondealing) with the problem of America's capital supply may be cited. A few days ago the American Academy of Political and Social Science published a new volume of its *Annals*, entirely devoted to the investigation of vital issues of the nation. The title of the volume is *Meaning of the 1952*

Presidential Election. To this symposium Professor Harold M. Groves of the University of Wisconsin contributed an article, "Are Taxes Too High?" The author comes out "with a largely negative answer." From our point of view, the most interesting feature of the article is the fact that it reaches this conclusion without even mentioning the effects which taxes on income, corporations, excess profits and estates have upon the maintenance and formation of capital. What economists have said about these problems either remained unknown to the author or he does not consider it worthy of an answer.

One does not misrepresent the economic ideas determining the course of American policies if one blames them for not being conscious of the role the supply of new capital plays in improving and expanding production. An instructive example has been provided by the conflict between the government and business concerning the adequacy of depreciation quotas under inflationary conditions. In all the agitated debates concerning profits, taxes and the height of wage rates the capital supply is hardly mentioned, if at all. In comparing American wage rates and standards of living with those of foreign countries, most authors and politicians fail to stress the differences in the per-head quotas of capital invested.

In the latest forty years American taxation more and more adopted methods which considerably slowed down the pace of capital accumulation. If it continues along this line, it will one day reach the point at which no further increase in capital will be possible, or even decumulation will set in. There is only one way open to stop this evolution in time and to spare this country the fate of England and France. One must substitute sound economic ideas for fables and illusions.

Scarcity of Capital

Up to this point I have employed the terms *capital shortage* and *scarcity of capital* without further explication and definition. This was quite sufficient as long as I dealt primarily with the conditions of countries whose capital supply appears as inadequate when compared with the supply in more advanced countries, especially in the economically most advanced country, the United States. But in examining American problems, a more searching interpretation of terms is required.

Strictly speaking, capital has always been scarce and will always be. The available supply of capital goods can never become so abundant that all projects, the execution of which could improve the material well-being of people, could be undertaken. If it were otherwise, mankind would live in the Garden of Eden and would not have to bother at all about production. Whatever the state of the capital supply may be, in this real world of ours there will always be business projects that cannot be launched because the capital they would require is employed for other enterprises, the products of which are more urgently asked for by the consumers. In every branch of industry there are limits beyond which the investment of additional capital does not pay. It does not pay because the capital goods concerned can find employment in the production of goods which are in the eyes of the buying public more valuable. If, other things being equal, the supply of capital increases, projects which hitherto could not be undertaken become profitable and are started. There is never a lack of investment opportunities. If there is lack of opportunities for profitable investment, the reason is that all the capital goods available have already been invested in profitable projects.

In speaking of the capital shortage of a country that is poorer than other countries one does not refer to this phenomenon of the general and perpetual shortage of capital. One merely compares the state of affairs in this individual country with that of other countries in which capital is more abundant. Looking upon India one may say: Here are a number of artisans producing with a total capital of ten thousand dollars products with the market value of, let us say, one million dollars. In an American factory with a capital equipment of one million dollars the same number of workers turn out products with the market value of 500 times as many dollars. Indian businessmen unfortunately lack the capital to make such investments. The consequence is that productivity per man is lower in India than in America, that the total amount of goods available for consumption is smaller and that the average Indian is poor when compared with the average American.

There is, especially under inflationary conditions, no reliable standard available that could be applied in measuring the degree of the scarcity of capital. Where it is impossible to compare a country's conditions with those of countries in which the supply of capital is more plentiful, as is the case with this country, only comparisons with the hypothetical size of the capital supply (as it would have been if certain things had not happened) are possible. There is in such a country no phenomenon that would present itself as capital scarcity so clearly and manifestly as the capital scarcity presents itself today to the people of India. All that can be said is: If in our nation people had saved more in the past, some improvements in technological methods (and lateral expansion of production by duplication of equipment of the kind already in existence for which the capital required is lacking) would have been feasible.

"Soak the Rich" Taxation

It is not easy to explain this state of affairs to people misled by the passionate anti-capitalistic agitation. As the self-styled intellectuals see it, the capitalist system and the greed of the businessmen are to blame for the fact that the total sum of products turned out for consumption is not greater than it actually is. The only way to do away with poverty they know is to take away—by means of progressive taxation—as much as possible from the well-to-do. In their eyes the wealth of the rich is the cause of the poverty of the poor. In accordance with this idea the fiscal policies of all nations and especially also of the United States were in the last decades directed toward confiscating ever-increasing portions of the wealth and income of the higher brackets. The greater part of the funds thus collected would have been employed by the taxpayers for saving and additional capital accumulation. Their investment would have increased productivity per man-hour and would in this way have provided more goods for consumption. It would have raised the average standard of living of the common man. If the government spends them for current expenditure, they are dissipated and capital accumulation is concomitantly slowed down.

Whatever one may think about the reasonableness of this policy of soaking the rich, it is impossible to deny the fact that it has already reached its limits. In Great Britain the Socialist Chancellor of the Exchequer had to admit a few years ago that even total confiscation of all that has still been left to people with higher incomes would add only a quite negligible sum to internal revenue and that there can no longer be any question of improving the lot of the indigent by taking it away from the rich.

In this country a total confiscation of incomes above twenty-five thousand dollars would at best yield much less than one billion dollars, a very small sum indeed when compared with the size of our present budget and the probable deficit. The main principle of the financial policies of the self-styled progressives has been pursued to the point at which it defeats itself and its absurdity becomes manifest. The progressives are at their wit's end. Henceforth, if they want to expand public expenditure further, they will have to tax more heavily precisely those classes of voters for whose support they have hitherto canvassed by placing the main burden upon the shoulders of the minority of wealthier people. (A very embarrassing dilemma indeed for the next Congress.)

To Raise Wages, Increase Capital Investment

But it is exactly the perplexity of this situation that offers a favorable opportunity for the substitution of sound economic principles for the pernicious errors that prevailed in the last decades. Now is the time to explain to the voters the causes of American prosperity on the one hand, and of the plight of the backward nations on the other hand. They must learn that what makes American wage rates much higher than those in other countries is the size of capital invested and that any further improvement of their standard of living depends on a sufficient accumulation of additional capital. Today only the businessmen worry about the provision of new capital for the expansion and improvement of their plants. The rest of the people are indifferent with regard to this issue, not knowing that their well-being and that of their children is at stake. What is needed is to make the importance of these problems understood by everybody. No party platform is to be considered as satisfactory that does not contain the following point: As the prosperity of the nation and the height of wage rates depend on a continual increase in the capital invested in its plants, mines and farms, it is one of the foremost tasks of good government to remove all obstacles that hinder the accumulation and investment of new capital.

ॐ PART 2

Money, Inflation, and Government

Nothing is inflationary except inflation, i.e., an increase in the quantity of money in circulation and credit subject to check (check-book money). And under present conditions nobody but the government can bring an inflation into being.

—"Wages, Unemployment, and Inflation"

4

Middle-of-the-Road Policy
Leads to Socialism

The Unpopularity of Capitalism

The fundamental dogma of all brands of socialism and communism is that the market economy or capitalism is a system that hurts the vital interests of the immense majority of people for the sole benefit of a small minority of rugged individualists. It condemns the masses to progressing impoverishment. It brings about misery, slavery, oppression, degradation and exploitation of the working men, while it enriches a class of idle and useless parasites.

This doctrine was not the work of Karl Marx. It had been developed long before Marx entered the scene. Its most successful propagators were not the Marxian authors, but such men as Carlyle and Ruskin, the British Fabians, the German professors and the American Institutionalists. And it is a very significant fact that the correctness of this dogma was contested only by a few economists who were very soon silenced and barred from access to the universities, the press, the leadership of political parties and, first of all, public office. Public opinion by and large accepted the condemnation of capitalism without any reservation.

Socialism

But, of course, the practical political conclusions which people drew from this dogma were not uniform. One group declared that there is but one way to wipe out these evils, namely to abolish capitalism entirely. They advocate the substitution of public control of the means of production for private control. They aim at the establishment of what

Address delivered before the University Club in New York, April 18, 1950. First printed by *Commercial and Financial Chronicle*, May 4, 1950.

is called socialism, communism, planning, or state capitalism. All these terms signify the same thing. No longer should the consumers, by their buying and abstention from buying, determine what should be produced, in what quantity and of what quality. Henceforth a central authority alone should direct all production activities.

Interventionism

A second group seems to be less radical. They reject socialism no less than capitalism. They recommend a third system, which, as they say, is as far from capitalism as it is from socialism, which as a third system of society's economic organization stands midway between the two other systems and, while retaining the advantages of both, avoids the disadvantages inherent in each. This third system is known as the system of interventionism. In the terminology of American politics it is often referred to as the middle-of-the-road policy.

What makes this third system popular with many people is the particular way they choose to look upon the problems involved. As they see it, two classes, the capitalists and entrepreneurs on the one hand and the wage earners on the other hand, are arguing about the distribution of the yield of capital and entrepreneurial activities. Both parties are claiming the whole cake for themselves. Now, suggest these mediators, let us make peace by splitting the disputed value equally between the two classes. The State as an impartial arbiter should interfere and should curb the greed of the capitalists and assign a part of the profits to the working classes. Thus it will be possible to dethrone the moloch capitalism without enthroning the moloch of totalitarian socialism.

Yet this mode of judging the issue is entirely fallacious. The antagonism between capitalism and socialism is not a dispute about the distribution of booty. It is a controversy about which of two schemes for society's economic organization, capitalism or socialism, is conducive to the better attainment of those ends which all people consider as the ultimate aim of activities commonly called economic, viz., the best possible supply of useful commodities and services. Capitalism wants to attain these ends by private enterprise and initiative, subject to the supremacy of the public's buying and abstention from buying on the market. The socialists want to substitute the unique plan of a central authority for the plans of the various individuals. They want to put in place of what Marx called the "anarchy of production" the exclusive monopoly of the government. The antagonism does not refer to the mode of distributing a fixed amount of amenities. It refers to the mode of producing all those goods which people want to enjoy. The conflict of the two principles is irreconcilable and does not allow of any compromise. Control is indivisible. Either the consumers' demand as manifested on the market decides for what purposes and how the factors of production should be employed, or the government takes care of these matters. There is nothing that could mitigate the opposition between these two contradictory principles. They preclude each other.

Interventionism is not a golden mean between capitalism and socialism. It is the design of a third system of society's economic organization and must be appreciated as such.

It is not the task of today's discussion to raise any questions about the merits either of capitalism or of socialism. I am dealing today with interventionism alone. And I do not intend to enter into an arbitrary evaluation of interventionism from any preconceived point of view. My only concern is to show how interventionism works and whether or not it can be considered as a pattern of a permanent system of society's economic organization.

The interventionists emphasize that they plan to retain private ownership of the means of production, entrepreneurship and market exchange. But, they go on to say, it is peremptory to prevent these capitalist institutions from spreading havoc and unfairly exploiting the majority of people. It is the duty of government to restrain, by orders and prohibitions, the greed of the propertied classes lest their acquisitiveness harms the poorer classes. Unhampered or laissez-faire capitalism is an evil. But in order to eliminate its evils, there is no need to abolish capitalism entirely. It is possible to improve the capitalist system by government interference with the actions of the capitalists and entrepreneurs. Such government regulation and regimentation of business is the only method to keep off totalitarian socialism and to salvage those features of capitalism which are worth preserving.

On the ground of this philosophy, the interventionists advocate a galaxy of various measures. Let us pick out one of them, the very popular scheme of price control.

Price Control

The government believes that the price of a definite commodity, e.g., milk, is too high. It wants to make it possible for the poor to give their children more milk. Thus it resorts to a price ceiling and fixes the price of milk at a lower rate than that prevailing on the free market. The result is that the marginal producers of milk, those producing at the highest cost, now incur losses. As no individual farmer or businessman can go on producing at a loss, these marginal producers stop producing and selling milk on the market. They will use their cows and their skill for other more profitable purposes. They will, for example, produce butter, cheese or meat. There will be less milk available for the consumers, not more. This, of course, is contrary to the intentions of the government. It wanted to make it easier for some people to buy more milk. But, as an outcome of its interference, the supply available drops. The measure proves abortive from the very point of view of the government and the groups it was eager to favor. It brings about a state of affairs, which—again from the point of view of the government—is even less desirable than the previous state of affairs which it was designed to improve.

Now, the government is faced with an alternative. It can abrogate its decree and refrain from any further endeavors to control the price of milk. But if it insists upon its intention to keep the price of milk below the rate the unhampered market would have determined and wants nonetheless to avoid a drop in the supply of milk, it must try to eliminate the causes that render the marginal producers' business unremunerative. It must add to the first decree concerning only the price of milk a second decree fixing the prices of the factors of production necessary for the production of milk at such a low rate that the marginal producers of milk will no longer suffer losses and will therefore abstain from restricting output. But then the same story repeats itself on a remoter plane. The supply of the factors of production required for the production of milk drops, and again the government is back where it started. If it does not want to admit defeat and to abstain from any meddling with prices, it must push further and fix the prices of those factors of production which are needed for the production of the factors necessary for the production of milk. Thus the government is forced to go further and further, fixing step by step the prices of all consumers' goods and of all factors of production—both human, i.e., labor, and material—and to order every entrepreneur and every worker to continue work at these prices and wages. No branch of industry can be omitted from this all-round fixing of prices and wages and from this obligation to produce those quantities which the government wants to see produced. If some branches were to be left free out of regard for the fact that they produce only goods qualified as non-vital or even as luxuries, capital and labor would tend to flow into them and the result would be a drop in the supply of those goods, the prices of which the government has fixed precisely because it considers them as indispensable for the satisfaction of the needs of the masses.

But when this state of all-round control of business is attained, there can no longer be any question of a market economy. No longer do the citizens by their buying and abstention from buying determine what should be produced and how. The power to decide these matters has devolved upon the government. This is no longer capitalism; it is all-round planning by the government, it is socialism.

Socialism, the German Pattern

It is, of course, true that this type of socialism preserves some of the labels and the outward appearance of capitalism. It maintains, seemingly and nominally, private ownership of the means of production, prices, wages, interest rates, and profits. In fact, however, nothing counts but the government's unrestricted autocracy. The government tells the entrepreneurs and capitalists what to produce and in what quantity and quality, at what prices to buy and from whom, at what prices to sell and to whom. It decrees at what wages and where the workers must work. Market exchange is but a sham. All the prices, wages and interest rates are determined by the authority. They are prices, wages and interest rates in appearance only; in fact they are merely quantity relations in the government's orders. The government, not the consumers, directs production. The government determines each citizen's income, it assigns to everybody the position in which he has to work. This is socialism in the outward guise of capitalism. It is the *Zwangswirtschaft* of Hitler's German Reich and the planned economy of Great Britain.

For the scheme of social transformation which I have depicted is not merely a theoretical construction. It is a realistic portrayal of the succession of events that brought about socialism in Germany, in Great Britain and in some other countries.

The Germans, in the First World War, began with price ceilings for a small group of consumers' goods considered as vital necessaries. It was the inevitable failure of these measures that impelled them to go further and further until, in the second period of the war, they designed the Hindenburg plan. In the context of the Hindenburg plan no room whatever was left for a free choice on the part of the consumers and for initiative action on the part of business. All economic activities were unconditionally subordinated to the exclusive jurisdiction of the authorities. The total defeat of the Kaiser swept the whole imperial apparatus of administration away and with it went also the grandiose plan. But when in 1931 Chancellor Brüning embarked anew on a policy of price control and his successors, first of all Hitler, obstinately clung to it, the same story repeated itself.

Socialism, the British Experience

Great Britain and all the other countries which in the First World War adopted measures of price control had to experience the same failure. They too were pushed further and further in their attempts to make the initial decrees work. But they were still at a rudimentary stage of this development when the victory and the opposition of the public brushed away all schemes for controlling prices.

It was different in the Second World War. Then Great Britain again resorted to price ceilings for a few vital commodities and had to run the whole gamut proceeding further and further until it had substituted all-round planning of the country's whole economy for economic freedom. When the war came to an end, Great Britain was a socialist commonwealth.

It is noteworthy to remember that British socialism was not an achievement of Mr. Attlee's Labor government, but of the war cabinet of Mr. Winston Churchill. What the Labor Party did was not the establishment of socialism in a free country, but retaining socialism as it had developed during the war in the postwar period. The fact has been obscured by the great sensation made about the nationalization of the Bank of England, the coal mines and other branches of business. However, Great Britain is to be called a socialist country not because certain enterprises have been formally expropriated and nationalized, but because all the economic activities of all citizens are subject to full control of the government and its agencies. The authorities direct the allocation of capital and of manpower to the various branches of business. They determine what should be produced. Supremacy in all business activities is exclusively vested in the government. The people are reduced to the status of wards, unconditionally bound to obey orders. To the businessmen, the former entrepreneurs, merely ancillary functions are left. All that they are free to do is to carry into effect, within a neatly circumscribed narrow field, the decisions of the government departments.

One Intervention Leads to Further Interventions

What we have to realize is that price ceilings affecting only a few commodities fail to attain the ends sought. On the contrary, they produce effects which from the point of view of the government are even worse than the previous state of affairs which the government wanted to alter. If the government, in order to eliminate these inevitable but unwelcome consequences, pursues its course further and further, it finally transforms the system of capitalism and free enterprise into socialism of the Hindenburg pattern.

The same is true of all other types of meddling with the market phenomena. Minimum wage rates, whether decreed and enforced by the government or by labor union pressure and violence, result in mass unemployment prolonged year after year as soon as they try to raise wage rates above the height of the unhampered market. The attempts to lower interest rates by credit expansion generate, it is true, a period of booming business. But the prosperity thus created is only an artificial hothouse product and must inexorably lead to the slump and to the depression. People must pay heavily for the easy-money orgy of a few years of credit expansion and inflation.

The recurrence of periods of depression and mass unemployment has discredited capitalism in the opinion of injudicious people. Yet these events are not the outcome of the operation of the free market. They are on the contrary the result of well-intentioned but ill-advised government interference with the market. There are no means by which the height of wage rates and the general standard of living can be raised other than by accelerating the increase of capital as compared with population. The only means to raise wage rates permanently for all those seeking jobs and eager to earn wages is to raise the productivity of the industrial effort by increasing the per-head quota of capital invested. What makes American wage rates by far exceed the wage rates of Europe and Asia is the fact that the American worker's toil and trouble is aided by more and better tools. All that good government can do to improve the material well-being of the people is to establish and to preserve an institutional order in which there are no obstacles to the progressing accumulation of new capital, required for the improvement of technological methods of production. This is what capitalism did achieve in the past and will achieve in the future too if not sabotaged by a bad policy.

Socialism by Intervention or Expropriation

Interventionism cannot be considered as an economic system destined to stay. It is a method for the transformation of capitalism into socialism by a series of successive steps. It is as such different from the endeavors of the communists to bring about socialism at one stroke. The difference does not refer to the ultimate end of the political movement; it refers mainly to the tactics to be resorted to for the attainment of an end that both groups are aiming at.

Karl Marx and Frederick Engels recommended successively each of these two ways for the realization of socialism. In 1848, in the *Communist Manifesto*, they outlined a plan for the step-by-step transformation of capitalism into socialism. The proletariat should be raised to the position of the ruling class and use its political supremacy "to wrest, by degrees, all capital from the bourgeoisie." This, they declare, "cannot be effected except by means of despotic inroads on the rights of property and on the conditions of bourgeois production; by means of measures, therefore, which appear economically insufficient and untenable, but which in the course of the movement outstrip themselves, necessitate further inroads upon the old social order, and are unavoidable as a means of entirely revolutionizing the mode of production." In this vein they enumerate by way of example ten measures.

In later years Marx and Engels changed their minds. In his main treatise, *Das Kapital*, first published in 1867, Marx saw things in a different way. Socialism is bound to come "with the inexorability of a law of nature." But it cannot appear before capitalism has reached its full maturity. There is but *one* road to the collapse of capitalism, namely the progressive evolution of capitalism itself. Then only will the great final revolt of the working class give it the finishing stroke and inaugurate the everlasting age of abundance.

From the point of view of this later doctrine Marx and the school of orthodox Marxism reject all policies that pretend to restrain, to regulate and to improve capitalism. Such policies, they declare, are not only futile, but outright harmful. For they rather delay the coming of age of capitalism, its maturity, and thereby also its collapse. They are therefore not progressive, but reactionary. It was this idea that led the German Social Democratic party to vote against Bismarck's social security legislation and to frustrate Bismarck's plan to nationalize the German tobacco industry. From the point of view of the same doctrine, the communists branded the American New Deal as a reactionary plot extremely detrimental to the true interests of the working people.

What we must realize is that the antagonism between the interventionists and the communists is a manifestation of the conflict between the two doctrines of the early Marxism and of the late Marxism. It is the conflict between the Marx of 1848, the author of the *Communist Manifesto*, and the Marx of 1867, the author of *Das Kapital*. And it is paradoxical indeed that the document in which Marx endorsed the policies of the present-day self-styled anti-communists is called the *Communist Manifesto*.

There are two methods available for the transformation of capitalism into socialism. One is to expropriate all farms, plants and shops and to operate them by a bureaucratic apparatus as departments of the government. The whole of society, says Lenin, becomes "one office and one factory, with equal work and equal pay,"* the whole economy will be organized "like the postal system."† The second method is the method of the Hindenburg plan, the originally German pattern of the welfare state and of planning. It forces every firm and every individual to comply strictly with the orders issued by the government's central board of production management. Such was the intention of the National Industrial Recovery Act of 1933 which the resistance of business frustrated and the Supreme Court declared unconstitutional. Such is the idea implied in the endeavors to substitute planning for private enterprise.

Socialism via Foreign Exchange Control

The foremost vehicle for the realization of this second type of socialism is in industrial countries like Germany and Great Britain foreign exchange control. These countries cannot feed and clothe their people out of domestic resources. They must import large quantities of food and raw materials. In order to pay for these badly needed imports, they

---

* Cf. Lenin, *State and Revolution*, Little Lenin Library No. 14, New York 1932, p. 84.
† Ibidem, p. 44.

must export manufactures, most of them produced out of imported raw material. In such countries almost every business transaction directly or indirectly is conditioned either by exporting or importing or by both exporting and importing. Hence the government's monopoly of buying and selling foreign exchange makes every kind of business activity depend on the discretion of the agency entrusted with foreign exchange control. In this country matters are different. The volume of foreign trade is rather small when compared with the total volume of the nation's trade. Foreign exchange control would only slightly affect the much greater part of American business. This is the reason why in the schemes of our planners there is hardly any question of foreign exchange control. Their pursuits are directed toward the control of prices, wages and interest rates, toward the control of investment, and the limitation of profits and incomes.

Effects of Progressive Taxation

Looking backward on the evolution of income tax rates from the beginning of the Federal income tax in 1913 until the present day, one can hardly expect that the tax will not one day absorb 100% of all surplus above the income of the average voter. It is this that Marx and Engels had in mind when in the *Communist Manifesto* they recommended "a heavy progressive or graduated income tax."

Another of the suggestions of the *Communist Manifesto* was "abolition of all right of inheritance." Now, neither in Great Britain nor in this country have the laws gone up to this point. But again, looking backward upon the past history of the estate taxes, we have to realize that they more and more have approached the goal set by Marx. Estate taxes of the height they have already attained for the upper brackets are no longer to be qualified as taxes. They are measures of expropriation.

The philosophy underlying the system of progressive taxation is that the income and the wealth of the well-to-do classes can be freely tapped. What the advocates of these tax rates fail to realize is that the greater part of the incomes taxed away would not have been consumed but saved and invested. In fact, this fiscal policy does not only prevent the further accumulation of new capital. It brings about capital decumulation. This is certainly today the state of affairs in Great Britain.

The Trend Toward Socialism

The course of events in the past thirty years shows a continuous although sometimes interrupted progress toward the establishment in this country of socialism of the British and German pattern. The U. S. embarked later than these two other countries upon this decline and is today still farther away from its end. But if the trend of this policy will not change, the final result will only in accidental and negligible points differ from what happened in the England of Attlee and in the Germany of Hitler. The middle-of-the-road policy is not an economic system that can last. It is a method for the realization of socialism by installments.

Many people object. They stress the fact that most of the laws which aim at planning or at expropriation by means of progressive taxation have left some loopholes which offer to private enterprise a margin within which it can go on. That such loopholes still exist and that thanks to them this country is still a free country is certainly true. But this loopholes capitalism is not a lasting system. It is a respite. Powerful forces are at work to close these loopholes. From day to day the field in which private enterprise is free to operate is narrowed down.

Of course, this outcome is not inevitable. The trend can be reversed as was the case with many other trends in history. The Marxian dogma according to which socialism is bound to come "with the inexorability of a law of nature" is just an arbitrary surmise devoid of any proof. But the prestige which this vain prognostic enjoys not only with the Marxians, but with many self-styled non-Marxians, is the main instrument of the progress of socialism. It spreads defeatism among those who otherwise would gallantly fight the socialist menace. The most powerful ally of Soviet Russia is the doctrine that the "wave of the future" carries us toward socialism and that it is therefore "progressive" to sympathize with all measures that restrict more and more the operation of the market economy.

Antidote to Socialism, Laissez Faire Ideology

Even in this country which owes to a century of "rugged individualism" the highest standard of living ever attained by any nation, public opinion condemns laissez-faire. In the last fifty years thousands of books have been published to indict capitalism and to advocate radical interventionism, the welfare state and socialism. The few books which tried to explain adequately the working of the free market economy were hardly noticed by the public. Their authors remained obscure, while such authors as Veblen, Commons, John Dewey and Laski were exuberantly praised. It is a well-known fact that the legitimate stage as well as the Hollywood industry are no less radically critical of free enterprise than are many novels. There are in this country many periodicals which in every issue furiously attack economic freedom. There is hardly any magazine of opinion that would plead for the system that supplied the immense majority of the people with good food and shelter, with cars, refrigerators, radio sets and other things which the subjects of other countries call luxuries.

The impact of this state of affairs is that practically very little is done to preserve the system of private enterprise. There are only middle-of-the-roaders who think they have been successful when they have delayed for some time an especially ruinous measure. They are always in retreat. They put up today with measures which only ten or twenty years ago they would have considered as undiscussable. They will in a few years acquiesce in other measures which they today consider as simply out of the question.

What can prevent the coming of totalitarian socialism is only a thorough change in ideologies. What we need is neither anti-socialism nor anti-communism but an open positive endorsement of that system to which we owe all the wealth that distinguishes our age from the comparatively straitened conditions of ages gone by.

5

Inflation and Price Control

Under Socialism, Government Controls; Under Capitalism, the Market Directs

Under socialism production is entirely directed by the orders of the central board of production management. The whole nation is an "industrial army" (a term used by Karl Marx in the *Communist Manifesto*) and each citizen is bound to obey his superior's orders. Everybody has to contribute his share to the execution of the overall plan adopted by the Government.

In the free economy no production czar tells a man what he should do. Everybody plans and acts for himself. The coordination of the various individuals' activities, and their integration into a harmonious system for supplying the consumers with the goods and services they demand, is brought about by the market process and the price structure it generates.

The market steers the capitalistic economy. It directs each individual's activities into those channels in which he best serves the wants of his fellow-men. The market alone puts the whole social system of private ownership of the means of production and free enterprise in order and provides it with sense and meaning.

There is nothing automatic or mysterious in the operation of the market. The only forces determining the continually fluctuating state of the market are the value judgments of the various individuals and their actions as directed by these value judgments. The ultimate factor in the market is the striving of each man to satisfy his needs and wants in the best possible way. Supremacy of the market is tantamount to the supremacy of the consumers. By their buying, and by their abstention from buying, the consumers determine not only the price structure,

The Commercial and Financial Chronicle, December 20, 1945.

but no less what should be produced and in what quantity and quality and by whom. They determine each entrepreneur's profit or loss, and thereby who should own the capital and run the plants. They make poor men rich and rich men poor. The profit system is essentially production for use, as profits can be earned only by success in supplying consumers in the best and cheapest way with the commodities they want to use.

Price Control Leads to Central Planning

From this it becomes clear what government tampering with the price structure of the market means. It diverts production from those channels into which the consumers want to direct it into other lines. Under a market not manipulated by government interference there prevails a tendency to expand the production of each article to the point at which a further expansion would not pay because the price realized would not exceed costs. If the government fixes a maximum price for certain commodities below the level which the unhampered market would have determined for them and makes it illegal to sell at the potential market price, production involves a loss for the marginal producers. Those producing with the highest costs go out of the business and employ their production facilities for the production of other commodities, not affected by price ceilings. The government's interference with the price of a commodity restricts the supply available for consumption. This outcome is contrary to the intentions which motivated the price ceiling. The government wanted to make it easier for people to obtain the article concerned. But its intervention results in shrinking of the supply produced and offered for sale.

If this unpleasant experience does not teach the authorities that price control is futile and that the best policy would be to refrain from any endeavors to control prices, it becomes necessary to add to the first measure, restricting merely the price of one or of several consumers' goods, further measures. It becomes necessary to fix the prices of the factors of production required for the production of the consumers' goods concerned. Then the same story repeats itself on a remoter plane. The supply of those factors of production whose prices have been limited shrinks. Then again the government must expand the sphere of its price ceilings. It must fix the prices of the secondary factors of production required for the production of those primary factors. Thus the government must go farther and farther. It must fix the prices of all consumers' goods and of all factors of production, both material factors and labor, and it must force every entrepreneur and every worker to continue production at these prices and wage rates. No branch of production must be omitted from this all-round fixing of prices and wages and this general order to continue production. If some branches were to be left free, the result would be a shifting of capital and labor to them and a corresponding fall in the supply of the goods whose prices the government has fixed. However, it is precisely these goods which the government considers as especially important for the satisfaction of the needs of the masses.

But when such a state of all-round control of business is achieved, the market economy has been replaced by a system of centralized planning, by socialism. It is no longer the consumers but the government who decides what should be produced and in what quantity and quality. The entrepreneurs are no longer entrepreneurs. They have been reduced to the status of shop managers—or *Betriebsführer*, as the Nazis said—and are bound to obey the orders issued by the government's central board of production management. The workers are bound to work in the plants to whom the authorities have assigned them; their wages are determined by authoritarian decrees. The government is supreme. It determines each citizen's income and standard of living. It is totalitarian.

Price control is contrary to purpose if it is limited to some commodities only. It cannot work satisfactorily within a market economy. The endeavors to make it work must needs enlarge the sphere of the commodities subject to price control until the prices of all commodities and services are regulated by authoritarian decree and the market ceases to work.

Either production can be directed by the prices fixed on the market by the buying or the abstention from buying on the part of the public; or it can be directed by the government's offices. There is no third solution available. Government control of a part of prices only results in a state of affairs which—without any exception—everybody considers as absurd and contrary to purpose. Its inevitable result is chaos and social unrest.

Price Control in Germany

It has been asserted again and again that German experience has proved that price control is feasible and can attain the ends sought by the government resorting to it. Nothing can be more erroneous.

When the First World War broke out, the German Reich immediately adopted a policy of inflation. To prevent the inevitable outcome of inflation, a general rise in prices, it resorted simultaneously to price control. The much-glorified efficiency of the German police succeeded rather well in enforcing these price ceilings. There were no black markets. But the supply of the commodities subject to price control quickly fell. Prices did not rise. But the public was no longer in a position to purchase food, clothes and shoes. Rationing was a failure. Although the government reduce more and more the rations allotted to each individual, only a few people were fortunate enough to get all that the ration card entitled them to. In their endeavors to make the price control system work, the authorities expanded step by step the sphere of the commodities subject to price control. One branch of business after the other was centralized and put under the management of a government commissary. The government obtained full control of all vital branches of production. But even this was not enough as long as other branches of industry were left free. Thus the government decided to go still farther. The Hindenburg Program aimed at all-round planning of all production. The idea was to entrust the direction of all business activities to the authorities. If the Hindenburg Program had been executed, it would have transformed Germany into a purely *totalitarian* commonwealth. It would have realized the ideal of Othmar Spann, the champion of "German" socialism, to make Germany a country in which private property exists only in a formal and legal sense, while in fact there is public ownership only.

However, the Hindenburg Program had not yet been completely put into effect when the Reich collapsed. The disintegration of the imperial bureaucracy brushed away the whole apparatus of price control and of war socialism. But the nationalist authors continued to extol the merits of the *Zwangswirtschaft*, the compulsory economy. It was, they said, the most perfect method for the realization of socialism in a predominantly industrial country like Germany. They triumphed when Chancellor Brüning in 1931 went back to the essential provisions of the Hindenburg Program and when later the Nazis enforced these decrees with the utmost brutality.

The Nazis did not, as their foreign admirers contend, enforce price control within a market economy. With them price control was only one device within the frame of an all-round system of central planning. In the Nazi economy there was no question of private initiative and free enterprise. All production activities were directed by the *Reichswirtschaftsministerium*. No enterprise was free to deviate in the conduct of its operations from the orders issued by the government. Price control was only a device in the complex of innumerable decrees and orders regulating the minutest details of every business activity and precisely fixing every individual's tasks on the one hand and his income and standard of living on the other.

What made it difficult for many people to grasp the very nature of the Nazi economic system was the fact that the Nazis did not expropriate the entrepreneurs and capitalists openly and that they did not adopt the principle of income equality which the Bolshevists espoused in the first years of Soviet rule and discarded only later. Yet the Nazis removed the bourgeois completely from control. Those entrepreneurs who were neither Jewish nor suspect of liberal and pacifist leanings retained their positions in the economic structure. But they were virtually merely salaried civil servants bound to comply unconditionally with the orders of their superiors, the bureaucrats of the Reich and the Nazi party. The capitalists got their (sharply reduced) dividends. But like other citizens they were not free to spend more of their incomes than the Party deemed as adequate to their status and rank in the hierarchy of graduated leadership. The surplus had to be invested in exact compliance with the orders of the Ministry of Economic Affairs.

The experience of Nazi Germany certainly did not disprove the statement that price control is doomed to failure within an economy not completely socialized. Those advocates of price control who pretend that they aim at preserving the system of private initiative and free enterprise are badly mistaken. What they really do is to paralyze the operation of the steering device of this system. One does not preserve a system by destroying its vital nerve; one kills it.

Inflation Is Monetary Expansion

Inflation is the process of a great increase in the quantity of money in circulation. Its foremost vehicle in continental Europe is the issue of non-redeemable legal tender banknotes. In this country inflation consists mainly in government borrowing from the commercial banks and also in an increase in the quantity of paper money of various types and of token coins. The government finances its deficit spending by inflation.

Inflation must result in a general tendency towards rising prices. Those into whose pockets the additional quantity of currency flows are in a position to expand their demand for vendable goods and services. An additional demand must, other things being equal, raise prices. No sophistry and no syllogisms can conjure away this inevitable consequence of inflation.

The semantic revolution which is one of the characteristic features of our day has obscured and confused this fact. The term inflation is used with a new connotation. What people today call inflation is not inflation, i.e., the increase in the quantity of money and money substitutes, but the general rise in commodity prices and wage rates which is the inevitable consequence of inflation. This semantic innovation is by no means harmless.

First of all there is no longer any term available to signify what inflation used to signify. It is impossible to fight an evil which you cannot name. Statesmen and politicians no longer have the opportunity to resort to a terminology accepted and understood by the public when they want to describe the financial policy they are opposed to. They must enter into a detailed analysis and description of this policy with full particulars and minute accounts whenever they want to refer to it, and they must repeat this bothersome procedure in every sentence in which they deal with this subject. As you cannot name the policy increasing the quantity of the circulating medium, it goes on luxuriantly.

The second mischief is that those engaged in futile and hopeless attempts to fight the inevitable consequences of inflation—the rise in prices—are masquerading their endeavors as a fight against inflation. While fighting the symptoms, they pretend to fight the root causes of the evil. And because they do not comprehend the causal relation between the increase in money in circulation and credit expansion on the one hand and the rise in prices on the other, they practically make things worse.

The best example is provided by the subsidies. As has been pointed out, price ceilings reduce supply because production involves a loss for the marginal producers. To prevent this outcome governments often grant subsidies to the farmers operating with the highest costs. These subsidies are financed out of additional credit expansion. Thus they result in increasing the inflationary pressure. If the consumers were to pay higher prices for the products concerned, no further inflationary effect would emerge. The consumers would have to use for such surplus payments only money which had been already put into circulation. Thus the allegedly brilliant idea to fight inflation by subsidies in fact brings about more inflation.

The Real Dangers of Inflation

There is practically no need today to enter into a discussion of the comparatively slight and harmless inflation that under a gold standard can be brought about by a great increase in gold production. The problems the world must face today are those of runaway inflation. Such an inflation is always the outcome of a deliberate government policy. The government is on the one hand not prepared to restrict its expenditure. On the other hand it does not want to balance its budget by taxes levied or by loans from the public. It chooses inflation because it considers it as the minor evil. It goes on expanding credit and increasing the quantity of money in circulation because it does not see what the inevitable consequences of such a policy must be.

There is no cause to be too much alarmed about the extent to which inflation has gone already in this country. Although it has gone very far and has done much harm, it has certainly not created an irreparable disaster. There is no doubt that the United States is still free to change its methods of financing and to return to a sound money policy.

The real danger does not consist in what has happened already, but in the spurious doctrines from which these events have sprung. The superstition that it is possible for the government to eschew the inexorable consequences of inflation by price control is the main peril. For this doctrine diverts the public's attention from the core of the problem. While the authorities are engaged in a useless fight against the attendant phenomena, only few people are attacking the source of the evil, the treasury's methods of providing for the enormous expenditures. While the bureaus make headlines with their activities, the statistical figures concerning the increase in the nation's currency are relegated to an inconspicuous place in the newspapers' financial pages.

Here again the example of Germany may stand as a warning. The tremendous German inflation which reduced in 1923 the purchasing power of the mark to one billionth of its prewar value was not an act of God. It would have been possible to balance Germany's postwar budget without resorting to the Reichsbank's printing press. The proof is that the Reich's budget was easily balanced as soon as the breakdown of the old Reichsbank forced the government to abandon its inflationary policy. But before this happened, all German would-be experts stubbornly denied that the rise in commodity prices, wage rates and foreign exchange rates had anything to do with the government's method of reckless spending. In their eyes only profiteering was to blame. They advocated thoroughgoing enforcement of price control as the panacea and called those recommending a change in financial methods "deflationists."

The German nationalists were defeated in the two most terrific wars of history. But the economic fallacies which pushed Germany into its nefarious aggressions unfortunately survive. The monetary errors developed by German professors such as Lexis and Knapp and put into effect by Havenstein, the Reichsbank's president in the critical years of its great inflation, are today the official doctrine of France and of many other European countries. There is no need for the United States to import these absurdities.

6

Economic Aspects of the Pension Problem

Workers Pay the Cost of Their Pension Benefits Themselves

Whenever a law or labor union pressure burdens the employers with
an additional expenditure for the benefit of the employees, people talk
of "social gains." The idea implied is that such benefits confer on the
employees a boon beyond the salaries or wages paid to them and that
they are receiving a grant which they would have missed in the absence of such a law or such a clause in the contract. It is assumed that
the workers are getting something for nothing.

This view is entirely fallacious. What the employer takes into account in considering the employment of additional hands or in dis-
charging a number of those already in his service, is always the value of
the services rendered or to be rendered by them. He asks himself: How
much does the employment of the man concerned add to the output?
Is it reasonable to expect that the expenditure caused by his employment will at least be recovered by the sale of the additional product
produced by his employment? If the answer to the second question is
in the negative, the employment of the man will cause a loss. As no enterprise can in the long run operate on a loss basis, the man concerned
will be discharged or, respectively, will not be hired.

In resorting to this calculation the employer takes into account not
only the individual's take-home wages, but all the costs of employing him. If, e.g., the government—as is the case in some European
countries—collects a percentage of each firm's total payroll as a tax
which the firm is strictly forbidden to deduct from wages paid to the
workers, the amount that enters into the calculation is: wages paid out
to the worker plus the quota of the tax. If the employer is bound to
provide for pensions, the sum entered into the calculation is: wages

The Commercial and Financial Chronicle, February 23, 1950.

paid out plus an allowance for the pension, computed according to actuarial methods.

The consequence of this state of affairs is that the incidence of all alleged "social gains" falls upon the wage-earner. Their effect does not differ from the effect of any kind of raise in wage rates.

On a free labor market wage rates tend toward a height at which all employers ready to pay these rates can find all the men they need and all the workers ready to work for this rate can find jobs. There prevails a tendency toward full employment. But as soon as the laws or the labor unions fix rates at a higher level, this tendency disappears. Then workers are discharged and there are job-seekers who cannot find employment. The reason is that at the artificially raised wage rates only the employment of a smaller number of hands pays. While on an unhampered labor market unemployment is only transitory, it becomes a permanent phenomenon when the governments or the unions succeed in raising wage rates above the potential market level. Even Lord Beveridge, about twenty years ago, admitted that the continuance of a substantial volume of unemployment is in itself the proof that the price asked for labor as wages is too high for the conditions of the market. And Lord Keynes, the inaugurator of the so-called "full employment policy," implicitly acknowledged the correctness of this thesis. His main reason for advocating inflation as a means to do away with unemployment was that he believed that gradual and automatic lowering of *real* wages as a result of rising prices would not be so strongly resisted by labor as any attempt to lower money wage rates.

What prevents the government and the unions from raising wage rates to a steeper height than they actually do is their reluctance to price out of the labor market too great a number of people. What the workers are getting in the shape of pensions payable by the employing corporation reduces the amount of wages that the unions can ask for without increasing unemployment. The unions in asking pensions for which the company has to pay without any contribution on the part of the beneficiaries have made a choice. They have preferred pensions to an increase in take-home wages. Economically it does not make any difference whether the workers do contribute or do not to the fund out of which the pensions will be paid. It is immaterial for the employer whether the cost of employing workers is raised by an increase in take-home wages or by the obligation to provide for pensions. For the worker, on the other hand, the pensions are not a free gift on the part of the employer. The pension claims they acquire restrict the amount of wages they could get without calling up the spectre of unemployment. Correctly computed, the income of a wage earner entitled to a pension consists of his wages plus the amount of the premium he would have to pay to an insurance company for the acquisition of an equivalent claim. Ultimately the granting of pensions amounts to a restriction of the wage earner's freedom to use his total income according to his own designs. He is forced to cut down his current consumption in order to provide for his old age. We may neglect dealing with the question whether such a restriction of the individual worker's freedom is expedient or not. What is important to emphasize is merely that the pensions are not a gift on the part of the employer. They are a disguised wage raise of a peculiar character. The employee is forced to use the increment for acquiring a pension.

The Same Government That Offers Pensions
Reduces Their Purchasing Power

It is obvious that the amount of the pension each man will be entitled to claim one day can only be fixed in terms of money. Hence the value of these claims is inextricably linked with the vicissitudes of the American monetary unit, the dollar.

The present Administration is eager to devise various schemes for old-age and disability pensions. It is intent upon extending the number of people included in the government's social security system and to increase the benefits under this system. It openly supports the demands of the unions for pensions to be granted by the companies without contribution on the part of the beneficiaries. But at the same time the same administration is firmly committed to a policy which is bound to lower more and more the purchasing power of the dollar. It has proclaimed unbalanced budgets and deficit spending as the first principle of public finance, as a new way of life. While hypocritically pretending to fight inflation, it has elevated boundless credit expansion and recklessly increased the amount of money in circulation to the dignity of an essential postulate of popular government and economic democracy.

Let nobody be fooled by the lame excuse that what is intended is not permanent deficits, but only the substitution of balancing the budget over a period of several years for balancing it every year. According to this doctrine in years of prosperity budgetary surpluses are to be accumulated which have to be balanced against the deficits incurred in years of depression. But what is to be considered as good business and what as bad business is left to the decision of the party in power. The Administration itself declared that the fiscal year 1949 was, in spite of a moderate recession near its end, a year of prosperity. But it did not accumulate a surplus in this year of prosperity; it produced a considerable deficit. Remember how the Democrats in the 1932 electoral campaign criticized the Hoover Administration for its financial shortcomings. But as soon as they came into office, they inaugurated their notorious schemes of pump-priming, deficit spending and so on.

What the doctrine of balancing budgets over a period of many years really means is this: As long as our own party is in office, we will enhance our popularity by reckless spending. We do not want to annoy our friends by cutting down expenditures. We want the voters to feel happy under the artificial short-lived prosperity which the easy money policy and a rich supply of additional money generate. Later, when our adversaries will be in office, the inevitable consequence of our expansionist policy, viz., depression, will appear. Then we shall blame them for the disaster and assail them for their failure to balance the budget properly.

It is very unlikely that the practice of deficit spending will be abandoned in the not too distant future. As a fiscal policy it is very convenient to inept governments. It is passionately advocated by hosts of pseudo-economists. It is praised at the universities as the most beneficial expedient of "unorthodox," really "progressive" and "anti-fascist" methods of public finance. A radical change of ideologies would be required to restore the prestige of sound fiscal procedures, today decried as "orthodox" and "reactionary." Such an overthrow of an almost universally accepted doctrine is unlikely to occur as long as the living generation of professors and politicians has not passed away. The present writer, having for more than forty years uncompromisingly fought against all varieties of credit expansion and inflation, is forced sadly to admit that the prospects for a speedy return to sound management of monetary affairs are rather thin. A realistic evaluation of the state of public opinion, the doctrines taught at the universities and the mentality of politicians and pressure groups must show us that the inflationist tendencies will prevail for many years.

The inevitable result of inflationary policies is a drop in the monetary unit's purchasing power. Compare the dollar of 1950 with the dollar of 1940! Compare the money of any European or American country with

its *nominal* equivalent a dozen or two dozen years ago! As an inflationary policy works only as long as the yearly increments in the amount of
money in circulation are increased more and more, the rise in prices
and wages and the corresponding drop in purchasing power will go on
at an accelerated pace. The experience of the French franc may give us
a rough image of the dollar thirty or forty years from today.

Now it is such periods of time that count for pension plans. The
present workers of the United States Steel Corporation will receive
their pensions in twenty, thirty or forty years. Today a pension of one
hundred dollars a month means a rather substantial allowance. What
will it mean in 1980 or 1990? Today, as the Welfare Commissioner of
the City of New York has shown, 52 cents can buy all the food a person
needs to meet the daily caloric and protein requirements. How much
will 52 cents buy in 1980?

Such is the issue. What the workers are aiming at in striving after
social security and pensions is, of course, security. But their "social
gain" withers away with the drop in the dollar's purchasing power.
In enthusiastically supporting the Fair Deal's fiscal policy, the union
members are themselves frustrating all their social security and pension schemes. The pensions they will be entitled one day to claim will
be a mere sham.

No solution can be found for this dilemma. In an industrial society all deferred payments must be stipulated in terms of money. They
shrink with the shrinking of the money's purchasing power. A policy of
deficit spending saps the very foundation of all interpersonal relations
and contracts. It frustrates all kinds of savings, social security benefits
and pensions.

Government Spending Is No Substitute for Capital Accumulation

How can it happen that the American workers fail to see that their policies are at cross purposes?

The answer is: they are deluded by the fallacies of what is called
"new economics." This allegedly new philosophy ignores the role of
capital accumulation. It does not realize that there is but one means
to increase wage rates for all those eager to get jobs and thereby to improve the standard of living, namely to accelerate the increase of capital as compared with population. It talks about technological progress
and productivity without being aware that no technological improvement can be achieved if the capital required is lacking. Just at the in-

stant in which it became obvious that the most serious obstacle to any farther economic betterment is, not only in the backward countries but also in England, the shortage of capital, Lord Keynes, enthusiastically supported by many American authors, advanced his doctrine of the evils of saving and capital accumulation. As these men see it, all that is unsatisfactory is caused by the inability of private enterprise to cope with the conditions of the "mature" economy. The remedy they recommend is simple indeed. The state should fill the gap. They blithely assume that the state has unlimited means at its disposal. The state can undertake all projects which are too big for private capital. There is simply nothing that would surpass the financial power of the government of the United States. The Tennessee Valley project and the Marshall Plan were just modest beginnings. There are still many valleys in America left for further action. And then there are many rivers in other parts of the globe. Only a short time ago Senator McMahon outlined a gigantic project that dwarfs the Marshall Plan. Why not? If it is unnecessary to adjust the amount of expenditure to the means available, there is no limit to the spending of the great god State.

It is no wonder that the common man falls prey to the illusions which dim the vision of dignified statesmen and learned professors. Like the expert advisers of the president, he entirely neglects to recognize the main problem of American business, viz., the insufficiency of the accumulation of new capital. He dreams of abundance while a shortage is threatening. He misinterprets the high profits which the companies report. He does not perceive that a considerable part of these profits are illusory, a mere arithmetical consequence of the fact that the sums laid aside as depreciation quotas are insufficient. These illusory profits, a phony result of the drop in the dollar's purchasing power, will be absorbed by the already risen costs of replacing the factories' worn-out equipment. Their ploughing back is not additional investment, it is merely capital maintenance. There is much less available for a substantial expansion of investment and for the improvement of technological methods than the misinformed public thinks.

Pension Benefits Depend on Capital and Investment

Looking backward fifty or a hundred years we observe a steady progress of America's ability to produce and thereby to consume. But it is a serious blunder to assume that this trend is bound to continue. This past progress has been effected by a speedy increase of capital accumulation. If the accumulation of new capital is slowed down or entirely ceases, there cannot be any question of further improvements.

Such is the real problem American labor has to face today. The problems of capital maintenance and the accumulation of new capital do not concern merely "management." They are vital for the wage earner. Exclusively preoccupied with wage rates and pensions, the unions boast of their Pyrrhic victories. The union members are not conscious of the fact that their fate is tied up with the flowering of their employers' enterprises. As voters they approve of a taxation system which taxes away and dissipates for current expenditure those funds which would have been saved and invested as new capital.

What the workers must learn is that the only reason why wage rates are higher in the United States than in other countries is that the per head quota of capital invested is higher. The psychological danger of all kinds of pension plans is to be seen in the fact that they obscure this point. They give to the workers an unfounded feeling of security. Now, they think, our future is safe. No need to worry any longer. The unions will win for us more and more social gains. An age of plenty is in sight.

Yet, the workers should be worried about the state of the supply of capital. They should be worried because the preservation and the further improvement of what is called "the American way of life" and "an American standard of living" depends on the maintenance and the further increase of the capital invested in American business.

A man who is forced to provide of his own account for his old age must save a part of his income or take out an insurance policy. This leads him to examine the financial status of the savings bank or the insurance company or the soundness of the bonds he buys. Such a man is more likely to get an idea of the economic problems of his country than a man whom a pension scheme seemingly relieves of all worries. He will get the incentive to read the financial page of his newspaper and will become interested in articles which thoughtless people skip. If he is keen enough, he will discover the flaw in the teachings of the "new economics." But the man who confides in the pension stipulated believes that all such issues are "mere theory" and do not affect him. He does not bother about those things on which his well-being depends because he ignores this dependence. As citizens such people are a liability. A nation cannot prosper if its members are not fully aware of the fact that what alone can improve their conditions is more and better production. And this can only be brought about by increased saving and capital accumulation.

7

Wages, Unemployment, and Inflation

Consumers Guide Production and Determine Prices and Wages

Our economic system—the market economy or capitalism—is a system of consumers' supremacy. The customer is sovereign; he is, says a popular slogan, "always right." Businessmen are under the necessity of turning out what the consumers ask for and they must sell their wares at prices which the consumers can afford and are prepared to pay. A business operation is a manifest failure if the proceeds from the sales do not reimburse the businessman for all he has expended in producing the article. Thus the consumers in buying at a definite price determine also the height of the wages that are paid to all those engaged in the industries.

It follows that an employer cannot pay more to an employee than the equivalent of the value the latter's work, according to the judgment of the buying public, adds to the merchandise. (This is the reason why the movie star gets much more than the charwoman.) If he were to pay more, he would not recover his outlays from the purchasers; he would suffer losses and would finally go bankrupt. In paying wages, the employer acts as a mandatory of the consumers, as it were. It is upon the consumers that the incidence of the wage payments falls. As the immense majority of the goods produced are bought and consumed by people who are themselves receiving wages and salaries, it is obvious that in spending their earnings the wage earners and employees themselves are foremost in determining the height of the compensation they and those like them will get.

Better Tools Help Workers Produce and Earn More

The buyers do not pay for the toil and trouble the worker took nor for the length of time he spent in working. They pay for the products. The better

Christian Economics, March 4, 1958.

the tools are which the worker uses in his job, the more he can perform in an hour, the higher is, consequently, his remuneration. What makes wages rise and renders the material conditions of the wage earners more satisfactory is improvement in the technological equipment. American wages are higher than wages in other countries because the capital invested per head of the worker is greater and the plants are thereby in the position to use the most efficient tools and machines. What is called the American way of life is the result of the fact that the United States has put fewer obstacles in the way of saving and capital accumulation than other nations. The economic backwardness of such countries as India consists precisely in the fact that their policies hinder both the accumulation of domestic capital and the investment of foreign capital. As the capital required is lacking, the Indian enterprises are prevented from employing sufficient quantities of modern equipment, are therefore producing much less per man-hour, and can only afford to pay wage rates which, compared with American wage rates, appear as shockingly low.

There is only one way that leads to an improvement of the standard of living for the wage-earning masses, viz., the increase in the amount of capital invested. All other methods, however popular they may be, are not only futile, but are actually detrimental to the well-being of those they allegedly want to benefit.

Raising Wages Artificially Causes Unemployment

The fundamental question is: is it possible to raise wage rates for all those eager to find jobs above the height they would have attained on an unhampered labor market?

Public opinion believes that the improvement in the conditions of the wage earners is an achievement of the unions and of various legislative measures. It gives to unionism and to legislation credit for the rise in wage rates, the shortening of hours of work, the disappearance of child labor, and many other changes. The prevalence of this belief made unionism popular and is responsible for the trend in labor legislation of the last two decades. As people think that they owe to unionism their high standard of living, they condone violence, coercion, and intimidation on the part of unionized labor and are indifferent to the curtailment of personal freedom inherent in the union-shop and closed-shop clauses. As long as these fallacies prevail upon the minds of the voters, it is vain to expect a resolute departure from the policies that are mistakenly called progressive.

Yet this popular doctrine misconstrues every aspect of economic reality. The height of wage rates at which all those eager to get jobs can be employed depends on the marginal productivity of labor. The more capital—other things being equal—is invested, the higher wages climb on the free labor market, i.e., on the labor market not manipulated by the government and the unions. At these market wage rates all those eager to employ workers can hire as many as they want. At these market wage rates all those who want to be employed can get a job. There prevails on a free labor market a tendency toward full employment. In fact, the policy of letting the free market determine the height of wage rates is the only reasonable and successful full-employment policy. If wage rates, either by union pressure and compulsion or by government decree, are raised above this height, lasting unemployment of a part of the potential labor force develops.

Credit Expansion May Lower Real Wages
Temporarily and Spark a "Boom"

These opinions are passionately rejected by the union bosses and their followers among politicians and the self-styled intellectuals. The panacea they recommend to fight unemployment is credit expansion and inflation, euphemistically called "an easy money policy."

As has been pointed out above, an addition to the available stock of capital previously accumulated makes a further improvement of the industries' technological equipment possible, thus raises the marginal productivity of labor and consequently also wage rates. But credit expansion, whether it is effected by issuing additional banknotes or by granting additional credits on bank accounts subject to check, does not add anything to the nation's wealth of capital goods. It merely creates the illusion of an increase in the amount of funds available for an expansion of production. Because they can obtain cheaper credit, people erroneously believe that the country's wealth has thereby been increased and that therefore certain projects that could not be executed before are now feasible. The inauguration of these projects enhances the demand for labor and for raw materials and makes wage rates and commodity prices rise. An artificial boom is kindled.

Under the conditions of this boom, nominal wage rates which before the credit expansion were too high for the state of the market and therefore created unemployment of a part of the potential labor force are no longer too high and the unemployed can get jobs again. However, this happens only because under the changed monetary and credit conditions prices are rising or, what is the same expressed in other words, the purchasing power of the monetary unit drops. Then the same amount of nominal wages, i.e., wage rates expressed in terms of money, means less in real wages, i.e., in terms of commodities that can be bought by the monetary unit. Inflation can cure unemployment only by curtailing the wage earner's *real* wages. But then the unions ask for a new increase in wages in order to keep pace with the rising cost of living and we are back where we were before, i.e., in a situation in which large-scale unemployment can only be prevented by a further expansion of credit.

This is what happened in this country as well as in many other countries in the last years. The unions, supported by the government, forced the enterprises to agree to wage rates that went beyond the potential market rates, i.e., the rates which the public was prepared to refund to the employers in purchasing their products. This would have inevitably resulted in rising unemployment figures. But the government policies tried to prevent the emergence of serious unemployment by credit expansion, i.e., inflation. The outcome was rising prices, renewed demands for higher wages and reiterated credit expansion; in short, protracted inflation.

Endless Inflation Leads to Disaster

But finally the authorities become frightened. They know that inflation cannot go on endlessly. If one does not stop in time the pernicious policy of increasing the quantity of money and fiduciary media, the nation's currency system collapses entirely. The monetary unit's purchasing power sinks to a point which for all practical purposes is not better than zero. This happened again and again, in this country with the Continental Currency in 1781, in France in 1796, in Germany in 1923. It is never too early for a nation to realize that inflation cannot be considered as a way of life and that it is imperative to return to sound monetary policies. In recognition of these facts the administration and the Federal Reserve authorities some time ago discontinued the policy of progressive credit expansion.

It is not the task of this short article to deal with all the consequences which the termination of inflationary measures brings about. We have only to establish the fact that the return to monetary stability does not *generate* a crisis. It only brings to light the malinvestments and other mistakes that were made under the hallucination of the illusory prosperity created by the easy money. People become aware of the faults committed and, no longer blinded by the phantom of cheap credit, begin to readjust their activities to the real state of the supply of material factors of production. It is this—certainly painful, but unavoidable—readjustment that constitutes the depression.

One of the unpleasant features of this process of discarding chimeras and returning to a sober estimate of reality concerns the height of wage rates. Under the impact of the progressive inflationary policy the union bureaucracy acquired the habit of asking at regular intervals for wage raises, and business, after some sham resistance, yielded. As a result these rates were at the moment too high for the state of the market and would have brought about a conspicuous amount of unemployment. But the ceaselessly progressive inflation very soon caught up with them. Then the unions asked again for new raises and so on.

It does not matter what kind of justification the unions and their henchmen advance in favor of their claims. The unavoidable effects of forcing the employers to remunerate work done at higher rates than those the consumers are willing to restore to them in buying the products are always the same: rising unemployment figures.

At the present juncture the unions try to take up the old, a hundred times refuted purchasing power fable. They declare that putting more money into the hands of the wage earners—by raising wage rates, by increasing the benefits to the unemployed and by embarking upon new public works—would enable the workers to spend more and thereby stimulate business and lead the economy out of the recession into prosperity. This is the spurious pro-inflation argument to make all people happy through printing paper bills. Of course, if the quantity of the circulating media is increased, those into whose pockets the new fictitious wealth comes—whether they are workers or farmers or any other kind of people—will increase their spending. But it is precisely this increase in spending that inevitably brings about a general tendency of all prices to rise or, what is the same expressed in a different way, a drop in the monetary unit's purchasing power. Thus the help that an inflationary action could give to the wage earners is only of a short duration. To perpetuate it, one would have to resort again and again to new inflationary measures. It is clear that this leads to disaster.

Public, Political, and Union Pressures Can Lead Government to Inflate

There is a lot of nonsense said about these things. Some people assert that wage raises are "inflationary." But they are not in themselves inflationary. Nothing is inflationary except inflation, i.e., an increase in the quantity of money in circulation and credit subject to check (check-book money). And under present conditions nobody but the government can bring an inflation into being. What the unions can generate by forcing the employers to accept wage rates higher than the potential market rates is not inflation and not higher commodity prices, but unemployment of a part of the people anxious to get a job. Inflation is a policy to which the government resorts in order to prevent the large-scale unemployment the unions' wage raising would otherwise bring about.

The dilemma which this country—and no less many other countries—has to face is very serious. The extremely popular method of raising wage rates above the height the unhampered labor market would have established would produce catastrophic mass unemployment if inflationary credit expansion were not to rescue it. But inflation has not only very pernicious social effects. It cannot go on endlessly without resulting in the complete breakdown of the whole monetary system.

Public opinion, entirely under the sway of the fallacious labor union doctrines, sympathizes more or less with the union bosses' demand for a considerable rise in wage rates. As conditions are today, the unions have the power to make the employers submit to their dictates. They can call strikes and, without being restrained by the authorities, resort with impunity to violence against those willing to work. They are aware of the fact that the enhancement of wage rates will increase the number of jobless. The only remedy they suggest is more ample funds for unemployment compensation and a more ample supply of credit, i.e., inflation. The government, meekly yielding to a misguided public opinion and worried about the outcome of the impending election campaign, has unfortunately already begun to reverse its attempts to return to a sound monetary policy. Thus we are again committed to the pernicious methods of meddling with the supply of money. We are going on with the inflation that with accelerated speed makes the purchasing power of the dollar shrink. Where will it end? This is the question which Mr. Reuther and all the rest never ask.

Only stupendous ignorance can call the policies adopted by the self-styled progressives "pro-labor" policies. The wage earner like every other citizen is firmly interested in the preservation of the dollar's purchasing power. If, thanks to his union, his weekly earnings are raised above the market rate, he must very soon discover that the upward movement in prices not only deprives him of the advantages he expected, but besides makes the value of his savings, of his insurance policy and of his pension rights dwindle. And, still worse, he may lose his job and will not find another.

All political parties and pressure groups protest that they are opposed to inflation. But what they really mean is that they do not like the unavoidable consequences of inflation, viz., the rise in living costs. Actually they favor all policies that necessarily bring about an increase in the quantity of the circulating media. They ask not only for an easy money policy to make the unions' endless wage boosting possible but also for more government spending and—at the same time—for tax abatement through raising the exemptions.

Duped by the spurious Marxian concept of irreconcilable conflicts between the interests of the social classes, people assume that the interests of the propertied classes alone are opposed to the unions' demand for higher wage rates. In fact, the wage earners are no less interested in a return to sound money than any other group or class. A lot has been said in the last months about the harm fraudulent officers have inflicted upon the union membership. But the havoc done to the workers by the unions' excessive wage boosting is much more detrimental.

It would be an exaggeration to contend that the tactics of the unions are the sole threat to monetary stability and to a reasonable economic policy. Organized wage earners are not the only pressure group whose claims menace today the stability of our monetary system. But they are the most powerful and most influential of these groups and the primary responsibility rests with them.

Well-being Depends on Savings and Capital Formation

Capitalism has improved the standard of living of the wage earners to an unprecedented extent. The average American family enjoys today amenities of which, only a hundred years ago, not even the richest nabobs dreamed. All this well-being is conditioned by the increase in savings and capital accumulated; without these funds that enable business to make practical use of scientific and technological progress the American worker would not produce more and better things per hour of work than the Asiatic coolies, would not earn more and would, like them, wretchedly live on the verge of starvation. All measures which—like our income and corporation tax system—aim at preventing further capital accumulation or even at capital decumulation are therefore virtually anti-labor and anti-social.

One further observation must still be made about this matter of saving and capital formation. The improvement of well-being brought about by capitalism made it possible for the common man to save and thus to become in a modest way himself a capitalist. A considerable part of the capital working in American business is the counterpart of the savings of the masses. Millions of wage earners own saving deposits, bonds and insurance policies. All these claims are payable in dollars and their worth depends on the soundness of the nation's money. To preserve the dollar's purchasing power is also from this point of view a vital interest of the masses. In order to attain this end, it is not enough to print upon the bank notes the noble maxim *In God We Trust.* One must adopt an appropriate policy.

8

The Gold Problem

Why have a monetary system based on gold? Because, as conditions are today and for the time that can be foreseen today, the gold standard alone makes the determination of money's purchasing power independent of the ambitions and machinations of governments, of dictators, of political parties, and of pressure groups. The gold standard alone is what the nineteenth-century freedom-loving leaders (who championed representative government, civil liberties, and prosperity for all) called "sound money."

The eminence and usefulness of the gold standard consists in the fact that it makes the supply of money depend on the profitability of mining gold, and thus checks large-scale inflationary ventures on the part of governments.

The gold standard did not fail. Governments deliberately sabotaged it, and still go on sabotaging it. But no government is powerful enough to destroy the gold standard so long as the market economy is not entirely suppressed by the establishment of socialism in every part of the world.

Governments believe that it is the gold standard's fault alone that their inflationary schemes not only fail to produce the expected benefits, but unavoidably bring about conditions that (also in the eyes of the rulers themselves and most of the people) are considered as much worse than the alleged or real evils they were designed to eliminate. Except for the gold standard, governments are told by pseudo-economists that they could make everybody perfectly prosperous. Let us test the three doctrines advanced for the support of this fable of government omnipotence.

Originally published in *The Freeman*, June 1965. Reprinted with permission from the Foundation for Economic Education.

The Fiction of Government Omnipotence

"The state is God," said Ferdinand Lassalle, the founder of the German socialist movement. As such, the state has the power to "create" unlimited quantities of money and thus to make everybody happy. Intrepid and clear-headed people branded such a policy of "creating" money as inflation. The official terminology calls it nowadays "deficit spending."

But whatever the name used in dealing with this phenomenon may be, its meaning is obvious. The government increases the quantity of money in circulation. Then a greater quantity of money "chases" (as a rather silly but popular way of talking about these problems says) a quantity of goods and services that has not been increased. The government's action did not add anything to the available amount of useful things and services. It merely made the prices paid for them soar.

If the government wishes to raise the income of some people, for example, government employees, it has to confiscate by taxation a part of some other people's incomes, and then distribute the amount collected to its employees or favored groups. Then the taxpayers are forced to restrict their spending, while the recipients of the higher salaries or benefits are increasing their spending to the same amount. There does not result a conspicuous change in the purchasing power of the monetary unit.

But if the government provides the money it wants for the payment of higher salaries by printing it or the granting of additional credits, the new money in the hands of these beneficiaries constitutes on the market an additional demand for the not-increased quantity of goods and services offered for sale. The unavoidable result is a general tendency of prices to rise.

Any attempts the governments and their propaganda offices make to conceal this concatenation of events are in vain. Deficit spending means increasing the quantity of money in circulation. That the official terminology avoids calling it inflation is of no avail whatever.

The government and its chiefs do not have the powers of the mythical Santa Claus. They cannot spend except by taking out of the pockets of some people for the benefit of others.

The "Cheap-Money" Fallacy

Interest is the difference in the valuation of present goods and future goods; it is the discount in the valuation of future goods as against that of present goods. Interest cannot be "abolished" as long as people prefer an apple available today to an apple available only in a year, in ten years, or in a hundred years.

The height of the originary rate of interest,* which is the main component of the market rate of interest as determined on the loan market, reflects the difference in the people's valuation of present and future satisfaction of needs. The disappearance of interest, that is, an interest rate of zero, would mean that people do not care a whit about satisfying any of their present wants and are *exclusively* intent upon satisfying their future wants, their wants of the later years, decades, and centuries to come. People would only save and invest and would not be consuming.

On the other hand, if people were to stop saving, that is, making any provision for the future, be it even the future of the tomorrow, and would not save at all and consume all capital goods accumulated by previous generations, the rate of interest would rise beyond any limits.

It is thus obvious that the height of the market rate of interest ultimately does not depend on the whims, fancies, and pecuniary interests of the personnel operating the government apparatus of coercion and compulsion, the much-referred-to "public sector" of the economy. But the government has the power to push the Federal Reserve System, and the banks subject to it, into a policy of cheap money. Then the banks are expanding credit. Underbidding the rate of interest as established on the not-manipulated loan market, they offer additional credit created out of nothing. Thus they are inescapably falsifying the businessmen's estimation of market conditions. Although the supply of capital goods (that can only be increased by additional saving) remained unchanged, the illusion of a richer supply of capital is conjured up. Business is induced to embark upon projects which a sober calculation, not misled by the cheap-money ventures, would have disclosed as mal-investments (over-investment in capital). The additional quantities of credit inundating the market make prices and wages soar. An artificial boom, a boom built entirely upon the illusions of ample and easy

---

* See "Originary Interest" in *Human Action* by Ludwig von Mises, pages 526–32 (fourth edition, Irvington-on-Hudson, N. Y.: Foundation for Economic Education, 1996).

money, develops. But such a boom cannot last. Sooner or later it must become clear that, under the illusions created by the credit expansion, business has embarked upon projects for the execution of which the real savings are not rich enough. When this mal-investment becomes visible, the boom collapses.

The depression that follows is the process of liquidating the errors committed in the excesses of the artificial boom; it is the return to calm reasoning and a reasonable conduct of affairs within the limits of the available supply of capital goods. It is a painful process, but it is a process of restoration of business health.

Credit expansion is not a nostrum to make people happy. The boom it engenders must inevitably lead to a debacle and unhappiness.

If it were really possible to substitute credit expansion (cheap money) for the accumulation of capital goods by saving, there would not be any poverty in the world. The economically backward nations would not have to complain about the insufficiency of their capital equipment. All they would have to do for the improvement of their conditions would be to expand money and credit more and more. No "foreign aid" schemes would have emerged. But in granting foreign aid to the backward nations, the American government implicitly acknowledges that credit expansion is no real substitute for genuine capital accumulation through saving.

The Failure of Minimum Wage Legislation and of Union Coercion

The height of wage rates is determined by the consumers' appraisal of the value the worker's labor adds to the value of the article available for sale. As the immense majority of the consumers are themselves earners of wages and salaries, this means that the determination of the compensation for work and services rendered is made by the same kind of people who are receiving these wages and salaries. The fat earnings of the movie star and the boxing champion are provided by the welders, street sweepers, and charwomen who attend the performances and matches.

An entrepreneur who would try to pay a hired man less than the amount this man's work adds to the value of the product would be priced out of the labor market by the competition of other entrepreneurs eager to earn money. On the other hand, no entrepreneur can pay more to his helpers than the amount the consumers are prepared to refund to him in buying the product. If he were to pay higher wages, he would suffer losses and would be ejected from the ranks of the businessmen.

Governments decreeing minimum wage laws above the level of the market rates restrict the number of hands that can find jobs. Such governments are producing unemployment of a part of the labor force. The same is true for what is euphemistically called "collective bargaining."

The only difference between the two methods concerns the apparatus enforcing the minimum wage. The government enforces its orders in resorting to policemen and prison guards. The unions "picket." They and their members and officials have acquired the power and the right to commit wrongs to person and property, to deprive individuals of the means of earning a livelihood, and to commit many other acts which no one can do with impunity.* Nobody is today in a position to disobey an order issued by a union. To the employers no other choice is left than either to surrender to the dictates of the unions or to go out of business.

But governments and unions are impotent against economic law. Violence can prevent the employers from hiring help at potential market rates, but it cannot force them to employ all those who are anxious to get jobs. The result of the governments' and the unions' meddling with the height of wage rates cannot be anything else than an incessant increase in the number of unemployed.

It is precisely to prevent this outcome that the government-manipulated banking systems of all Western nations are resorting to inflation. Increasing the quantity of money in circulation and thereby lowering the purchasing power of the monetary unit, they are cutting down the oversized payrolls to a height consonant with the state of the market. This is today called Keynesian full-employment policy. It is in fact a method to perpetuate by continued inflation the futile attempts of governments and labor unions to meddle with the conditions of the labor market. As soon as the progress of inflation has adjusted wage rates so far as to avoid a spread of unemployment, government and unions resume with renewed zeal their ventures to raise wage rates above the level at which every job-seeker can find a job.

The experience of this age of the New Deal, the Fair Deal, the New Frontier, and the Great Society confirms the fundamental thesis of the true British lovers of political liberty in the nineteenth century, namely, that there is but one means to improve the material conditions of all of

---

* Cf. Roscoe Pound, *Legal Immunities of Labor Unions*, Washington, D.C., 1957, page 21.

the wage earners, viz., to increase the per-head quota of real capital invested. This result can only be brought about by additional saving and capital accumulation, never by government decrees, labor-union violence and intimidation, and inflation. The foes of the gold standard are wrong also in this regard.

The Inescapable Consequence, Namely, the United States Government Gold Holdings Will Shrink

In many parts of the earth an increasing number of people realize that the United States and most of the other nations are firmly committed to a policy of progressing inflation. They have learned enough from the experience of the recent decades to conclude that on account of these inflationary policies an ounce of gold will one day become more expensive in terms both of the currency of the United States and of their own country. They are alarmed and would like to avoid being victimized by this outcome.

Americans are forbidden to own gold coins and gold ingots.* Their attempts to protect their financial assets consist in the methods that the Germans in the most spectacular inflation that history knows called *Flucht in die Sachwerte* (flight into real values). They are investing in common stocks and real estate, and prefer to have debts payable in legal tender money rather than holding claims payable in it.

Even in the countries in which people are free to buy gold there are up to now no conspicuous purchases of gold on the part of financially potent individuals and institutions. Up to the moment at which French agencies began to buy gold, the buyers of gold were mostly people with modest incomes anxious to keep a few gold coins as a reserve for rainy days. It was the purchases via the London gold market on the part of such people that reduced the gold holdings of the United States.

❧

There is only one method available to prevent a further reduction of the American gold reserve, namely, radical abandonment of deficit spending as well as of any kind of "easy-money" policy.

---

* [Editor's note: In 1933, U.S. citizens were denied the right to own gold coins and gold ingots. They regained that right in January 1976.]

PART 3

Mises: Critic of Inflationism and Socialism

No effusions of authors however brilliant and sophisticated can alter the perennial economic laws. They are and work and take care of themselves.
  —"Lord Keynes and Say's Law"

Tyranny is the political corollary of socialism, as representative government is the political corollary of the market economy.
  —"Liberty and Its Antithesis"

9

Benjamin M. Anderson Challenges the Philosophy of the Pseudo-Progressives

The Two Lines of Marxian Thought and Policies

In all countries which have not openly adopted a policy of outright and all-round socialization the conduct of government affairs has been for many decades in the hands of statesmen and parties who style themselves "progressives" and scorn their opponents as "reactionaries." These progressives become sometimes (but not always) very angry if somebody calls them Marxians. In this protest they are right insofar as their tenets and policies are contrary to some of the Marxian doctrines and their application to political action. But they are wrong insofar as they unreservedly endorse the fundamental dogmas of the Marxian creed and act accordingly. While calling in question the ideas of Marx, the champion of integral revolution, they subscribe to piecemeal revolution.

For there are in the writings of Marx two distinct sets of theorems incompatible with each other: the line of the integral revolution as upheld in earlier days by Kautsky and later by Lenin, and the "reformist" line of revolution by instalments as vindicated by Sombart in Germany and the Fabians in England.

Common to both lines is the unconditional damnation of capitalism and its political "superstructure," representative government. Capitalism is described as a ghastly system of exploitation. It heaps riches upon a constantly diminishing number of "expropriators" and condemns the masses to increasing misery, oppression, slavery and degradation. But it is precisely this awkward system which "with the inexorability of a law of nature" finally brings about salvation. The coming of socialism is inevitable. It will appear as the result of the actions of the class-conscious proletarians. The "people" will finally triumph. All machinations of the wicked "bourgeois" are doomed to failure.

Originally published in *Plain Talk*, February 1950. Reprinted with permission from the Foundation for Economic Education.

But here the two lines diverge.

In the *Communist Manifesto* Marx and Engels designed a plan for the step-by-step transformation of capitalism into socialism. The proletarians should "win the battle of democracy" and thus raise themselves to the position of the ruling class. Then they should use their political supremacy to wrest, "by degrees," all capital from the bourgeoisie. Marx and Engels give rather detailed instructions for the various measures to be resorted to. It is unnecessary to quote in extenso their battle plan. Its diverse items are familiar to all Americans who have lived through the years of the New Deal and the Fair Deal. It is more important to remember that the fathers of Marxism themselves characterized the measures they recommended as "despotic inroads on the rights of property and the conditions of bourgeois production" and as "measures which appear economically insufficient and untenable, but which in the course of the movement outstrip themselves, necessitate further inroads upon the old social order, and are unavoidable as a means of entirely revolutionizing the mode of production." *

It is obvious that all the "reformers" of the last one hundred years were dedicated to the execution of the scheme drafted by the authors of the *Communist Manifesto* in 1848. In this sense Bismarck's *Sozialpolitik* as well as Roosevelt's New Deal have a fair claim to the epithet Marxian.

But on the other hand Marx also conceived a doctrine radically different from that expounded in the *Manifesto* and absolutely incompatible with it. According to this second doctrine "no social formation ever disappears before all the productive forces are developed for the development of which it is broad enough, and new higher methods of production never appear before the material conditions of their existence have been hatched out in the womb of the previous society." Full maturity of capitalism is the indispensable prerequisite for the appearance of socialism. There is but one road toward the realization of socialism, namely, the progressive evolution of capitalism itself which, through the incurable contradictions of the capitalist mode of production, causes its own collapse. Independently of the wills of men this

---

* It is important to realize that the words "necessitate further inroads upon the old social order" are lacking in the original German text of the *Manifesto* as well as in the later authorized German editions. They were inserted in 1888 by Engels into the translation by Samuel Moore which was published with the subtitle: "Authorized English Translation, edited and annotated by Frederick Engels."

process "executes itself through the operation of the inherent laws of capitalist production."

The utmost concentration of capital by a small cluster of expropriators on the one hand and unendurable impoverishment of the exploited masses on the other hand are the factors that alone can give rise to the great revulsion which will sweep away capitalism. Only then will the patience of the wretched wage earners give way and with a sudden stroke they will in a violent revolution overthrow the "dictatorship" of the bourgeoisie grown old and decrepit.

From the point of view of this doctrine Marx distinguishes between the policies of the petty bourgeois and those of the class-conscious proletarians. The petty bourgeois in their ignorance put all their hopes upon reforms. They are eager to restrain, to regulate and to improve capitalism. They do not see that all such endeavors are doomed to failure and make things worse, not better. For they delay the evolution of capitalism and thereby the coming of its maturity which alone can bring about the great debacle and thus deliver mankind from the evils of exploitation. But the proletarians, enlightened by the Marxian doctrine, do not indulge in these reveries. They do not embark upon idle schemes for an improvement of capitalism. They, on the contrary, recognize in every progress of capitalism, in every impairment of their own conditions and in every new recurrence of economic crisis a progress toward the inescapable collapse of the capitalist mode of production. The essence of their policies is to organize and to discipline their forces, the militant battalions of the people, in order to be ready when the great day of the revolution dawns.

This rejection of petty-bourgeois policies refers also to traditional labor union tactics. The plans of the workers to raise, within the framework of capitalism, wage rates and their standards of living through unionization and through strikes are vain. For the inescapable tendency of capitalism, says Marx, is not to raise but to lower the average standard of wages. Consequently he advised the unions to change their policies entirely. "Instead of the *conservative* motto: *A fair day's wage for a fair day's work*, they ought to inscribe on their banner the *revolutionary* watchword: *Abolition of the wages system*."

It is impossible to reconcile these two varieties of Marxian doctrines and of Marxian policies. They preclude one another. The authors of the *Communist Manifesto* in 1848 recommended precisely those policies which their later books and pamphlets branded as petty-bourgeois nonsense. Yet they never repudiated their scheme of 1848. They arranged new editions of the *Manifesto*. In the preface of the 1872 edition they declared that the principles for political action as outlined in 1848 need to be improved, as such practical measures must be always adjusted to changing historical conditions. But they did not, in this preface, stigmatize such reforms as the outcome of petty-bourgeois mentality. Thus the dualism of the two Marxian lines remained.

It was in perfect agreement with the intransigent revolutionary line that the German Social-Democrats in the eighties voted in the Reichstag against Bismarck's social security legislation and that their passionate opposition frustrated Bismarck's intention to socialize the German tobacco industry. It is no less consonant with this revolutionary line that the Stalinists and their henchmen describe the American New Deal and the Keynesian patent medicines as clever but idle contrivances designed to salvage and to preserve capitalism.

The present-day antagonism between the Communists on the one hand and the Socialists, New Dealers, and Keynesians on the other hand is a controversy about the means to be resorted to for the attainment of a goal common to both of these factions, namely the establishment of all-round central planning and the entire elimination of the market economy. It is a feud between two factions both of which are right in referring to the teachings of Marx. And it is paradoxical indeed that in this controversy the *anti-Communists'* title to the appellation "Marxian" is vested in the document called the *Communist Manifesto*.

The Guide of the Progressives

It is impossible to understand the mentality and the policy of the progressives if one does not take into account the fact that the *Communist Manifesto* is for them both manual and holy writ, the only reliable source of information about mankind's future as well as the ultimate code of political conduct. The *Communist Manifesto* is the only piece of the writings of Marx which they have really perused. Apart from the *Manifesto* they know only a few sentences out of context and without any bearing on the problems of current policies. But from the *Manifesto* they have learned that the coming of socialism is inevitable and will transform the earth into a Garden of Eden. They call themselves progressives and their opponents reactionaries precisely because, fighting for the bliss that is bound to come, they are borne by the "wave of the future" while their adversaries are committed to the hopeless attempt to stop the wheel of Fate and History. What a comfort to know that one's own cause is destined to conquer!

Then the progressive professors, writers, politicians, and civil servants discover in the *Manifesto* a passage which especially flatters their vanity. They belong to that "small section of the ruling class," to that "portion of the bourgeois ideologists" who have gone over to the proletariat, "the class that holds the future in its hands." Thus they are members of that elite "who have raised themselves to the level of comprehending theoretically the historical movements as a whole."

Still more important is the fact that the *Manifesto* provides them with an armor which makes them proof against all criticisms levelled against their policies. The bourgeois describe these progressive policies as "economically insufficient and untenable" and think that they have thereby demonstrated their inadequacy. How wrong they are! In the eyes of the progressives the excellence of these policies consists in the very fact that they are "economically insufficient and untenable." For exactly such policies are, as the *Manifesto* says, "unavoidable as a means of entirely revolutionizing the mode of production."

The *Communist Manifesto* serves as a guidebook not only to the personnel of the ever-swelling hosts of bureaucrats and pseudo-economists. It reveals to the "progressive" authors the very nature of the "bourgeois class culture." What a disgrace is this so-called bourgeois civilization! Fortunately the eyes of the self-styled "liberal" writers have been opened wide by Marx. The *Manifesto* tells them the truth about the unspeakable meanness and depravity of the bourgeoisie. Bourgeois marriage is "in fact a system of community of women." The bourgeois "sees in his wife a mere instrument of production." Our bourgeois, "not content with having the wives and daughters of their proletarians at their disposal, not to speak of common prostitutes, take the greatest pleasure in seducing each other's wives." In this vein innumerable plays and novels portray the conditions of the rotten society of decaying capitalism.

How different are conditions in the country whose proletarians, the vanguard of what the great Fabians, Sidney and Beatrice Webb, called the *New Civilization,* have already "liquidated" the exploiters! It may be granted that the Russian methods cannot be considered in *every* respect as a pattern to be adopted by the "liberals" of the West. It may also be true that the Russians, properly irritated by the machinations of the Western capitalists who are unceasingly plotting for a violent overthrow of the Soviet regime, become angry and sometimes give vent to their indignation in unfriendly language. Yet the fact remains that in Russia the word of the *Communist Manifesto* has become flesh. While under capitalism "the workers have no country" and "have nothing to lose but their chains," Russia is the true fatherland of all proletarians of the entire world. In a purely technical and legal sense it may be wrong for an American or Canadian to hand over confidential state documents or the secret designs of new weapons to the Russian authorities. From a higher point of view it may be understandable.

Anderson's Fight Against Destructionism

Such was the ideology that got hold of the men who in the last decades controlled the administration and determined the course of American affairs. It was against such a mentality that the economists had to fight in criticizing the New Deal.

Foremost among these dissenters was Benjamin McAlester Anderson. Throughout most of these fateful years he was the editor and sole author, first of the *Chase Economic Bulletin* (issued by the Chase National Bank), and then of the *Economic Bulletin* (issued by the Capital Research Company). In his brilliant articles he analyzed the policies when they were still in the state of development and then later again when their disastrous consequences had appeared. He raised his warning voice when there was still time to abstain from inadequate measures, and later he was never at a loss to show how the havoc which had been done by rejecting his previous objections and suggestions could be reduced as much as possible.

His criticism was never merely negative. He was always intent upon indicating roads which could lead out of an impasse. His was a constructive mind.

Anderson was not a doctrinaire remote from contact with reality. In his capacity as the economist of the Chase National Bank (from 1919 to 1939) he had ample opportunity to learn everything about American economic conditions. His familiarity with European business and politics was not surpassed by any other American. He knew intimately all the men who were instrumental in the conduct of national and international banking, business and politics. An indefatigable student, he was well acquainted with the content of state documents, statistical re-

ports and many confidential papers. His information was always complete and up-to-date.

But his most eminent qualities were his inflexible honesty, his unhes-
itating sincerity and his unflinching patriotism. He never yielded. He
always freely enunciated what he considered to be true. If he had been
prepared to suppress or only to soften his criticism of popular but ob-
noxious policies, the most influential positions and offices would have
been offered to him. But he never compromised. This firmness marks
him as one of the outstanding characters in this age of the supremacy
of time-servers.

His criticism of the easy money policy, of credit expansion and inflation, of the abandonment of the gold standard, of unbalanced budgets, of Keynesian spending, of price control, of subsidies, of silver purchases, of the tariff and many other similar expedients was crushing.
The apologists of these nostrums did not have the remotest idea how
to refute his objections. All they did was to dismiss Anderson as "orthodox." Although the undesired effects of the "unorthodox" policies he
had assailed never failed to appear exactly as he had predicted, almost
nobody in Washington paid any heed to his words.

The reason is obvious. The essence of Anderson's criticism was that
all these measures were "economically insufficient and untenable,"
that they were "despotic inroads" on the conditions of production, that
they "necessitate further inroads" and that they must finally destroy
our whole economic system. But these were just the ends which the
Washington Marxians were aiming at. They did not bother about sabotaging all essential institutions of capitalism, for in their eyes capitalism was the worst of all evils and was doomed anyway by the inexorable
laws of historical evolution. Their plan was to bring about, step by step,
the welfare state of central planning. In order to attain this goal they
had adopted the "untenable" policies which the *Communist Manifesto*
had declared to be "unavoidable as a means of entirely revolutionizing
the mode of production."

Anderson never tired of pointing out that the attempts to lower the
rate of interest by means of credit expansion must result in an artificial
boom and its inevitable aftermath, depression. In this vein he had attacked, long before 1929, the easy money policy of the twenties, and
later again, long before the breakdown of 1937, the New Deal's pump-
priming. He preached to deaf ears. For his opponents had learned

from Marx that the recurrence of depressions is a necessary outcome of the absence of central planning and cannot be avoided where there is "anarchy of production." The heavier the crisis may be, the nearer it brings the day of salvation when socialism will be substituted for capitalism.

The policy of keeping wage rates, either by government decree or by union violence and intimidation, above the height the unhampered labor market would have determined creates mass unemployment prolonged year after year. In dealing with American conditions as well as with those of Great Britain and other European countries, Anderson again and again referred to this economic law which, as even Lord Beveridge had asserted a few years before, is not contested by any competent authority. His arguments did not impress those who paraded as "friends of labor." They considered private enterprise's alleged "inability to provide jobs for all" as inevitable and were resolved to use mass unemployment as a lever for the realization of their designs.

If one wants to repulse the onslaughts of the Communists and Socialists and to shield Western civilization from Sovietization, it is not enough to disclose the abortiveness and impropriety of the progressive policies allegedly aiming at improving the economic conditions of the masses. What is needed is a frontal attack upon the whole web of Marxian, Veblenian, and Keynesian fallacies. As long as the syllogisms of these pseudo-philosophies retain their undeserved prestige, the average intellectual will go on blaming capitalism for all the disastrous effects of anti-capitalist schemes and devices.

Anderson's Posthumous Economic History

Benjamin Anderson devoted the last years of his life to the composition of a great book, the financial and economic history of our age of wars and progressing disintegration of civilization.

The most eminent historical works have come from authors who wrote the history of their own time for an audience contemporary with the events recorded. When gloom began to descend on the glory of Athens, one of its best citizens dedicated himself to Clio. Thucydides wrote the history of the Peloponnesian Wars and of the fateful direction of Athenian politics not merely as an unaffected student. His keen mind had fully recognized the disastrous significance of the course his countrymen were steering. He had been himself in politics and in the fighting forces. In writing history he wanted to serve his fellow-citizens. He wanted to admonish and to warn them, to stop their march toward the abyss.

Such also were the intentions of Anderson. He did not write merely for the sake of recording. His history is in some way also a continuation and recapitulation of his critical examination and interpretation of current events as provided by his *Bulletins* and other papers. It does not chronicle a dead past. It deals with forces which are still operating and spreading ruin. Like Thucydides, Anderson was eager to serve those who desire an exact knowledge of the past as a key to the future.

Like Thucydides, too, Anderson unfortunately did not live to see his book published. After his premature death, much lamented by all his friends and admirers, the D. Van Nostrand Company published it, with a preface by Henry Hazlitt, under the title *Economics and the Public Welfare, Financial and Economic History of the United States, 1914–1946*. It contains more than this title indicates. For the economic and financial history of the United States in this period was so closely intertwined with that of all other nations that his narrative embraces the whole orbit of Western civilization. The chapters dealing with British and French affairs are without doubt the best that has been said about the decline of these once flourishing countries.

It is very difficult for a reviewer to select from the treasure of information, wisdom and keen economic analysis assembled in this volume the most precious gems. The discriminating reader is captivated from the first page on and will not put it aside before he has reached the last page.

There are people who think that economic history neglects what they call the "human angle." Now, the proper field of economic history is prices and production, money and credit, taxes and budgets, and other such phenomena. But all these things are the outcome of human volitions and actions, plans and ambitions. The topic of economic history is man with all his knowledge and ignorance, his truth and his errors, his virtues and his vices.

Let us quote one of Anderson's observations. In commenting upon America's abandonment of the gold standard he remarks: "There is no need in human life so great as that men should trust one another and should trust their government, should believe in promises, and should keep promises in order that future promises may be believed in and in order that confident cooperation may be possible. Good faith—

personal, national, and international—is the first prerequisite of decent living, of the steady going on of industry, of governmental financial strength, and of international peace" (pages 317–18).

Such were the ideas that prompted the self-styled progressives to depreciate Anderson as "orthodox," "old-fashioned," "reactionary" and "Victorian." Sir Stafford Cripps, who twelve times solemnly denied that he would ever change the official relation of the pound against dollars and then, when he had done so, protested that he *naturally* could not admit such intention, is more to their liking.

10

Lord Keynes and Say's Law

I

Lord Keynes's main contribution did not lie in the development of new ideas but "in escaping from the old ones," as he himself declared at the end of the preface to his "General Theory." The Keynesians tell us that his immortal achievement consists in the entire refutation of what has come to be known as Say's Law of Markets. The rejection of this law, they declare, is the gist of all Keynes's teachings; all other propositions of his doctrine follow with logical necessity from this fundamental insight and must collapse if the futility of his attack on Say's Law can be demonstrated.*

Now it is important to realize that what is called Say's Law was in the first instance designed as a refutation of doctrines popularly held in the ages preceding the development of economics as a branch of human knowledge. It was not an integral part of the new science of economics as taught by the Classical economists. It was rather a preliminary—the exposure and removal of garbled and untenable ideas which dimmed people's minds and were a serious obstacle to a reasonable analysis of conditions.

Whenever business turned bad, the average merchant had two explanations at hand: the evil was caused by a scarcity of money and by general overproduction. Adam Smith, in a famous passage in "The Wealth of ations," exploded the first of these myths. Say devoted himself predominantly to a thorough refutation of the second.

As long as a definite thing is still an economic good and not a "free good," its supply is not, of course, *absolutely* abundant. There are still

Originally published in *The Freeman*, October 30, 1950. Reprinted with permission from the Foundation for Economic Education.
* P. M. Sweezy in *The New Economics*, ed. by S. E. Harris, New York, 1947, p. 105.

unsatisfied needs which a larger supply of the good concerned could satisfy. There are still people who would be glad to get more of this good than they are really getting. With regard to economic goods there can never be *absolute* overproduction. (And economics deals only with economic goods, not with free goods such as air which are no object of purposive human action, are therefore not produced, and with regard to which the employment of terms like underproduction and overproduction is simply nonsensical.)

With regard to economic goods there can be only *relative* overproduction. While the consumers are asking for definite quantities of shirts and of shoes, business has produced, say, a larger quantity of shoes and a smaller quantity of shirts. This is not general overproduction of all commodities. To the overproduction of shoes corresponds an underproduction of shirts. Consequently the result cannot be a general depression of all branches of business. The outcome is a change in the exchange ratio between shoes and shirts. If, for instance, previously one pair of shoes could buy four shirts, it now buys only three shirts. While business is bad for the shoemakers, it is good for the shirtmakers. The attempts to explain the general depression of trade by referring to an allegedly general overproduction are therefore fallacious.

Commodities, says Say, are ultimately paid for not by money, but by other commodities. Money is merely the commonly used medium of exchange; it plays only an intermediary role. What the seller wants ultimately to receive in exchange for the commodities sold is other commodities. Every commodity produced is therefore a price, as it were, for other commodities produced. The situation of the producer of any commodity is improved by any increase in the production of other commodities. What may hurt the interests of the producer of a definite commodity is his failure to anticipate correctly the state of the market. He has overrated the public's demand for his commodity and underrated its demand for other commodities. Consumers have no use for such a bungling entrepreneur; they buy his products only at prices which make him incur losses, and they force him, if he does not in time correct his mistakes, to go out of business. On the other hand, those entrepreneurs who have better succeeded in anticipating the public demand earn profits and are in a position to expand their business activities. This, says Say, is the truth behind the confused assertions of businessmen that the main difficulty is not in producing but in selling. It would be more appropriate to declare that the first and main problem of business is to produce in the best and cheapest way those commodities which will satisfy the most urgent of the not yet satisfied needs of the public.

Thus Smith and Say demolished the oldest and most naïve explanation of the trade cycle as provided by the popular effusions of inefficient traders. True, their achievement was merely negative. They exploded the belief that the recurrence of periods of bad business was caused by a scarcity of money and by a general overproduction. But they did not give us an elaborated theory of the trade cycle. The first explanation of this phenomenon was provided much later by the British Currency School.

The important contributions of Smith and Say were not entirely new and original. The history of economic thought can trace back some essential points of their reasoning to older authors. This in no way detracts from the merits of Smith and Say. They were the first to deal with the issue in a systematic way and to apply their conclusions to the problem of economic depressions. They were therefore also the first against whom the supporters of the spurious popular doctrine directed their violent attacks. Sismondi and Malthus chose Say as the target of passionate volleys when they tried—in vain—to salvage the discredited popular prejudices.

II

Say emerged victoriously from his polemics with Malthus and Sismondi. He proved his case, while his adversaries could not prove theirs. Henceforth, during the whole rest of the nineteenth century, the acknowledgment of the truth contained in Say's Law was the distinctive mark of an economist. Those authors and politicians who made the alleged scarcity of money responsible for all ills and advocated inflation as the panacea were no longer considered economists but "monetary cranks."

The struggle between the champions of sound money and the inflationists went on for many decades. But it was no longer considered a controversy between various schools of economists. It was viewed as a conflict between economists and anti-economists, between reasonable men and ignorant zealots. When all civilized countries had adopted the gold standard or the gold-exchange standard, the cause of inflation seemed to be lost forever.

Economics did not content itself with what Smith and Say had taught about the problems involved. It developed an integrated system of theorems which cogently demonstrated the absurdity of the inflationist sophisms. It depicted in detail the inevitable consequences of an increase in the quantity of money in circulation and of credit expansion. It elaborated the monetary or circulation credit theory of the business cycle which clearly showed how the recurrence of depressions of trade is caused by the repeated attempts to "stimulate" business through credit expansion. Thus it conclusively proved that the slump, whose appearance the inflationists attributed to an insufficiency of the supply of money, is on the contrary the necessary outcome of attempts to remove such an alleged scarcity of money through credit expansion.

The economists did not contest the fact that a credit expansion in its initial stage makes business boom. But they pointed out how such a contrived boom must inevitably collapse after a while and produce a general depression. This demonstration could appeal to statesmen intent on promoting the enduring well-being of their nation. It could not influence demagogues who care for nothing but success in the impending election campaign and are not in the least troubled about what will happen the day after tomorrow. But it is precisely such people who have become supreme in the political life of this age of wars and revolutions. In defiance of all the teachings of the economists, inflation and credit expansion have been elevated to the dignity of the first principle of economic policy. Nearly all governments are now committed to reckless spending and finance their deficits by issuing additional quantities of unredeemable paper money and by boundless credit expansion.

The great economists were harbingers of new ideas. The economic policies they recommended were at variance with the policies practiced by contemporary governments and political parties. As a rule many years, even decades, passed before public opinion accepted the new ideas as propagated by the economists and before the required corresponding changes in policies were effected.

It was different with the "new economics" of Lord Keynes. The policies he advocated were precisely those which almost all governments, including the British, had already adopted many years before his "General Theory" was published. Keynes was not an innovator and champion of new methods of managing economic affairs. His contribution consisted rather in providing an apparent justification for the policies which were popular with those in power in spite of the fact that all economists viewed them as disastrous. His achievement was a rationalization of the policies already practiced. He was not a "revolutionary," as some of his adepts called him. The "Keynesian revolution" took place long before Keynes approved of it and fabricated a pseudo-scientific justification for it. What he really did was to write an apology for the prevailing policies of governments.

This explains the quick success of his book. It was greeted enthusiastically by the governments and the ruling political parties. Especially enraptured were a new type of intellectuals, the "government economists." They had had a bad conscience. They were aware of the fact that they were carrying out policies which all economists condemned as contrary to purpose and disastrous. Now they felt relieved. The "new economics" reestablished their moral equilibrium. Today they are no longer ashamed of being the handymen of bad policies. They glorify themselves. They are the prophets of the new creed.

III

The exuberant epithets which these admirers have bestowed upon his work cannot obscure the fact that Keynes did not refute Say's Law. He rejected it emotionally, but he did not advance a single tenable argument to invalidate its rationale.

Neither did Keynes try to refute by discursive reasoning the teachings of modern economics. He chose to ignore them, that was all. He never found any word of serious criticism against the theorem that increasing the quantity of money cannot effect anything else than, on the one hand, to favor some groups at the expense of other groups, and, on the other hand, to foster capital malinvestment and capital decumulation. He was at a complete loss when it came to advancing any sound argument to demolish the monetary theory of the trade cycle. All he did was to revive the self-contradictory dogmas of the various sects of inflationism. He did not add anything to the empty presumptions of his predecessors, from the old Birmingham School of Little Shilling Men down to Silvio Gesell. He merely translated their sophisms—a hundred times refuted—into the questionable language of mathematical economics. He passed over in silence all the objections which such men as Jevons, Walras and Wicksell—to name only a few—opposed to the effusions of the inflationists.

It is the same with his disciples. They think that calling "those who fail to be moved to admiration of Keynes's genius" such names as "dullard" or "narrow-minded fanatic"* is a substitute for sound economic reasoning. They believe that they have proved their case by dismissing their adversaries as "orthodox" or "neo-classical." They reveal the utmost ignorance in thinking that their doctrine is correct because it is new.

In fact, inflationism is the oldest of all fallacies. It was very popular long before the days of Smith, Say and Ricardo, against whose teachings the Keynesians cannot advance any other objection than that they are old.

IV

The unprecedented success of Keynesianism is due to the fact that it provides an apparent justification for the "deficit spending" policies of contemporary governments. It is the pseudo-philosophy of those who can think of nothing else than to dissipate the capital accumulated by previous generations.

Yet no effusions of authors however brilliant and sophisticated can alter the perennial economic laws. They are and work and take care of themselves. Notwithstanding all the passionate fulminations of the spokesmen of governments, the inevitable consequences of inflationism and expansionism as depicted by the "orthodox" economists are coming to pass. And then, very late indeed, even simple people will discover that Keynes did not teach us how to perform the "miracle . . . of turning a stone into bread,"† but the not at all miraculous procedure of eating the seed corn.‡

---

* Professor G. Haberler, ["The General Theory," in *The New Economics*, ibid.,] p. 161
† Keynes, ["Proposals for an International Clearing Union," in *The New Economics*, ibid.,] p. 332.
‡ See Henry Hazlitt, *The Failure of the "New Economics*," chapter 3 on "Keynes vs. Say's Law," pp. 32–43. Arlington House, New Rochelle, New York, 1959.

See also Clarence B. Carson, "Permanent Depression," *The Freeman*, December 1979, volume 29, no. 12, pp. 743–51. The Foundation for Economic Education, Inc., Irvington-on-Hudson, New York.

11

Stones into Bread, the Keynesian Miracle

I

The stock-in-trade of all Socialist authors is the idea that there is potential plenty and that the substitution of socialism for capitalism would
make it possible to give to everybody "according to his needs." Other
authors want to bring about this paradise by a reform of the monetary
and credit system. As they see it, all that is lacking is more money and
credit. They consider that the rate of interest is a phenomenon artificially created by the man-made scarcity of the "means of payment." In
hundreds, even thousands, of books and pamphlets they passionately
blame the "orthodox" economists for their reluctance to admit that inflationist and expansionist doctrines are sound. All evils, they repeat
again and again, are caused by the erroneous teachings of the "dismal
science" of economics and the "credit monopoly" of the bankers and
usurers. To unchain money from the fetters of "restrictionism," to create free money (*Freigeld*, in the terminology of Silvio Gesell) and to
grant cheap or even gratuitous credit, is the main plank in their political platform.

Such ideas appeal to the uninformed masses. And they are very popular with governments committed to a policy of increasing the quantity
both of money in circulation and of deposits subject to check. However, the inflationist governments and parties have not been ready to
admit openly their endorsement of the tenets of the inflationists. While
most countries embarked upon inflation and on a policy of easy money,
the literary champions of inflationism were still spurned as "monetary
cranks." Their doctrines were not taught at the universities.

Originally published in *Plain Talk*, March 1948, as "The Keynesian Miracle." Reprinted with
permission from the Foundation for Economic Education.

John Maynard Keynes, late economic adviser to the British government, is the new prophet of inflationism. The "Keynesian Revolution" consisted in the fact that he openly espoused the doctrines of Silvio Gesell. As the foremost of the British Gesellians, Lord Keynes adopted also the peculiar messianic jargon of inflationist literature and introduced it into official documents. Credit expansion, says the *Paper of the British Experts* of April 8, 1943, performs the "miracle . . . of turning a stone into bread."* The author of this document was, of course, Keynes. Great Britain has indeed traveled a long way to this statement from Hume's and Mill's views on miracles.

II

Keynes entered the political scene in 1920 with his book, *The Economic Consequences of the Peace*. He tried to prove that the sums demanded for reparations were far in excess of what Germany could afford to pay and to "transfer." The success of the book was overwhelming. The propaganda machine of the German nationalists, well entrenched in every country, was busily representing Keynes as the world's most eminent economist and Great Britain's wisest statesman.

Yet it would be a mistake to blame Keynes for the suicidal foreign policy that Great Britain followed in the interwar period. Other forces, especially the adoption of the Marxian doctrine of imperialism and "capitalist warmongering," were of incomparably greater importance in the rise of appeasement. With the exception of a small number of keen-sighted men, all Britons supported the policy which finally made it possible for the Nazis to start the Second World War.

A highly gifted French economist, Étienne Mantoux, has analyzed Keynes's famous book point for point. The result of his very careful and conscientious study is devastating for Keynes the economist and statistician, as well as Keynes the statesman. The friends of Keynes are at a loss to find any substantial rejoinder. The only argument that his friend and biographer, Professor E. A. G. Robinson, could advance is that this powerful indictment of Keynes's position came "as might have been expected, from a Frenchman." (*Economic Journal*, vol. LVII, p. 23.) As if the disastrous effects of appeasement and defeatism had not affected Great Britain also!

---

* [Editor's note: Reprinted as "Proposals for an International Clearing Union," in *The New Economics*, ed. Seymour E. Harris (New York: Knopf, 1947), p. 332.]

Étienne Mantoux, son of the famous historian Paul Mantoux, was the most distinguished of the younger French economists. He had already made valuable contributions to economic theory—among them a keen critique of Keynes's *General Theory*, published in 1937 in the *Revue d'Économie Politique*—before he began his *The Carthaginian Peace or the Economic Consequences of Mr. Keynes* (Oxford University Press, 1946). He did not live to see his book published. As an officer in the French forces he was killed on active service during the last days of the war. His premature death was a heavy blow to France, which is today badly in need of sound and courageous economists.

III

It would be a mistake, also, to blame Keynes for the faults and failures of contemporary British economic and financial policies. When he began to write, Britain had long since abandoned the principle of *laissez-faire*. That was the achievement of such men as Thomas Carlyle and John Ruskin and, especially, of the Fabians. Those born in the eighties of the nineteenth century and later were merely epigones of the university and parlor Socialists of the late Victorian period. They were no critics of the ruling system, as their predecessors had been, but apologists of government and pressure group policies whose inadequacy, futility and perniciousness became more and more evident.

Professor Seymour E. Harris has just published a stout volume of collected essays by various academic and bureaucratic authors dealing with Keynes's doctrines as developed in his *General Theory of Employment, Interest and Money*, published in 1936. The title of the volume is *The New Economics, Keynes' Influence on Theory and Public Policy* (Alfred A. Knopf, New York, 1947). Whether Keynesianism has a fair claim to the appellation "*new* economics" or whether it is not, rather, a rehash of often-refuted Mercantilist fallacies and of the syllogisms of the innumerable authors who wanted to make everybody prosperous by fiat money, is unimportant. What matters is not whether a doctrine is new, but whether it is sound.

The remarkable thing about this symposium is that it does not even attempt to refute the *substantiated* objections raised against Keynes by serious economists. The editor seems to be unable to conceive that any honest and uncorrupted man could disagree with Keynes. As he sees it, opposition to Keynes comes from "the vested interests of scholars in the older theory" and "the preponderant influence of press, radio, finance and subsidized research." In his eyes, non-Keynesians are just a bunch of bribed sycophants, unworthy of attention. Professor Harris thus adopts the methods of the Marxians and the Nazis, who preferred to smear their critics and to question their motives instead of refuting their theses.

A few of the contributions are written in dignified language and are reserved, even critical, in their appraisal of Keynes's achievements. Others are simply dithyrambic outbursts. Thus Professor Paul A. Samuelson tells us: "To have been born as an economist before 1936 was a boon—yes. But not to have been born too long before!" And he proceeds to quote Wordsworth:

> Bliss was it in that dawn to be alive,
> But to be young was very heaven!

Descending from the lofty heights of Parnassus into the prosaic valleys of quantitative science, Professor Samuelson provides us with exact information about the susceptibility of economists to the Keynesian gospel of 1936. Those under the age of 35 fully grasped its meaning after some time; those beyond 50 turned out to be quite immune, while economists in-between were divided. After thus serving us a warmed-over version of Mussolini's *giovanezza* theme, he offers more of the outworn slogans of fascism, e.g., the "wave of the future." However, on this point another contributor, Mr. Paul M. Sweezy, disagrees. In his eyes Keynes, tainted by "the shortcomings of bourgeois thought" as he was, is not the savior of mankind, but only the forerunner whose historical mission it is to prepare the British mind for the acceptance of pure Marxism and to make Great Britain ideologically ripe for full socialism.

IV

In resorting to the method of innuendo and trying to make their adversaries suspect by referring to them in ambiguous terms allowing of various interpretations, the camp-followers of Lord Keynes are imitating their idol's own procedures. For what many people have admiringly called Keynes's "brilliance of style" and "mastery of language" were, in fact, cheap rhetorical tricks.

Ricardo, says Keynes, "conquered England as completely as the Holy Inquisition conquered Spain." This is as vicious as any compari-

son could be. The Inquisition, aided by armed constables and execu-
tioners, beat the Spanish people into submission. Ricardo's theories
were accepted as correct by British intellectuals without any pressure
or compulsion being exercised in their favor. But in comparing the two
entirely different things, Keynes obliquely hints that there was something shameful in the success of Ricardo's teachings and that those
who disapprove of them are as heroic, noble and fearless champions of
freedom as were those who fought the horrors of the Inquisition.

The most famous of Keynes's *aperçus* is: "Two pyramids, two masses
for the dead, are twice as good as one; but not so two railways from
London to York." It is obvious that this sally, worthy of a character in a
play by Oscar Wilde or Bernard Shaw, does not in any way prove the
thesis that digging holes in the ground and paying for them out of savings "will increase the real national dividend of useful goods and services." But it puts the adversary in the awkard position of either leaving
an apparent argument unanswered or of employing the tools of logic
and discursive reasoning against sparkling wit.

Another instance of Keynes's technique is provided by his mali-
cious description of the Paris Peace Conference. Keynes disagreed
with Clemenceau's ideas. Thus, he tried to ridicule his adversary by
broadly expatiating upon his clothing and appearance which, it seems,
did not meet with the standard set by London outfitters. It is hard to
discover any connection with the German reparations problem in the
fact that Clemenceau's boots "were of thick black leather, very good,
but of a country style, and sometimes fastened in front, curiously, by a
buckle instead of laces." After 15 million human beings had perished
in the war, the foremost statesmen of the world were assembled to give
mankind a new international order and lasting peace—and the British
Empire's financial expert was amused by the rustic style of the French
prime minister's footwear.

Fourteen years later there was another international conference.
This time Keynes was not a subordinate adviser, as in 1919, but one of
the main figures. Concerning this London World Economic Conference of 1933, Professor Robinson observes: "Many economists the world
over will remember . . . the performance in 1933 at Covent Garden in
honour of the Delegates of the World Economic Conference, which
owed its conception and organization very much to Maynard Keynes."

Those economists who were not in the service of one of the lamentably inept governments of 1933 and therefore were not delegates

and did not attend the delightful ballet evening will remember the London Conference for other reasons. It marked the most spectacular failure in the history of international affairs of those policies of neo-Mercantilism which Keynes backed. Compared with this fiasco of 1933, the Paris Conference of 1919 appears to have been a highly successful affair. But Keynes did not publish any sarcastic comments on the coats, boots and gloves of the delegates of 1933.

V

Although Keynes looked upon "the strange, unduly neglected prophet Silvio Gesell" as a forerunner, his own teachings differ considerably from those of Gesell. What Keynes borrowed from Gesell as well as from the host of other pro-inflation propagandists was not the content of their doctrine, but their practical conclusions and the tactics they applied to undermine their opponents' prestige. These stratagems are:

(a) All adversaries, that is, all those who do not consider credit expansion as the panacea, are lumped together and called *orthodox*. It is implied that there are no differences between them.

(b) It is assumed that the evolution of economic science culminated in Alfred Marshall and ended with him. The findings of modern subjective economics are disregarded.

(c) All that economists from David Hume on down to our time have done to clarify the results of changes in the quantity of money and money substitutes is simply ignored. Keynes never embarked upon the hopeless task of refuting these teachings by ratiocination.

In all these respects the contributors to the symposium adopt their master's technique. Their critique aims at a body of doctrine created by their own illusions, which has no resemblance to the theories expounded by serious economists. They pass over in silence all that economists have said about the inevitable outcome of credit expansion. It seems as if they have never heard anything about the monetary theory of the trade cycle.

For a correct appraisal of the success which Keynes's *General Theory* found in academic circles, one must consider the conditions prevailing in university economics during the period between the two world wars.

Among the men who occupied chairs of economics in the last few decades, there have been only a few genuine economists, i.e., men fully conversant with the theories developed by modern subjective economics. The ideas of the old classical economists, as well as those of the modern economists, were caricatured in the textbooks and in the classrooms; they were called such names as old-fashioned, orthodox, reactionary, bourgeois or Wall Street economics. The teachers prided themselves on having refuted for all time the abstract doctrines of Manchesterism and *laissez-faire*.

The antagonism between the two schools of thought had its practical focus in the treatment of the labor union problem. Those economists disparaged as orthodox taught that a permanent rise in wage rates for all people eager to earn wages is possible only to the extent that the per capita quota of capital invested and the productivity of labor increases. If—whether by government decree or by labor union pressure—minimum wage rates are fixed at a higher level than that at which the unhampered market would have fixed them, unemployment results as a permanent mass phenomenon.

Almost all professors of the fashionable universities sharply attacked this theory. As these self-styled "unorthodox" doctrinaires interpreted the economic history of the last two hundred years, the unprecedented rise in real wage rates and standards of living was caused by labor unionism and government pro-labor legislation. Labor unionism was, in their opinion, highly beneficial to the true interests of all wage-earners and of the whole nation. Only dishonest apologists of the manifestly unfair interests of callous exploiters could find fault with the violent acts of the unions, they maintained. The foremost concern of popular government, they said, should be to encourage the unions as much as possible and to give them all the assistance they needed to combat the intrigues of the employers and to fix wage rates higher and higher.

But as soon as the governments and legislatures had vested the unions with all the powers they needed to enforce their minimum wage rates, the consequences appeared which the "orthodox" economists had predicted; unemployment of a considerable part of the potential labor force was prolonged year after year.

The "unorthodox" doctrinaires were perplexed. The only argument they had advanced against the "orthodox" theory was the appeal to their own fallacious interpretation of experience. But now events developed precisely as the "abstract school" had predicted. There was confusion among the "unorthodox."

It was at this moment that Keynes published his *General Theory*.

What a comfort for the embarrassed "progressives"! Here, at last, they had something to oppose to the "orthodox" view. The cause of unemployment was not the inappropriate labor policies, but the shortcomings of the monetary and credit system. No need to worry any longer about the insufficiency of savings and capital accumulation and about deficits in the public household. On the contrary. The only method to do away with unemployment was to increase "effective demand" through public spending financed by credit expansion and inflation.

The policies which the *General Theory* recommended were precisely those which the "monetary cranks" had advanced long before and which most governments had espoused in the depression of 1929 and the following years. Some people believe that Keynes's earlier writings played an important part in the process which converted the world's most powerful governments to the doctrines of reckless spending, credit expansion and inflation. We may leave this minor issue undecided. At any rate it cannot be denied that the governments and peoples did not wait for the *General Theory* to embark upon these "Keynesian"—or more correctly, Gesellian policies.

VI

Keynes's *General Theory* of 1936 did not inaugurate a new age of economic policies; rather, it marked the end of a period. The policies which Keynes recommended were already then very close to the time when their inevitable consequences would be apparent and their continuation would be impossible. Even the most fanatical Keynesians do not dare to say that present-day England's distress is an effect of too much saving and insufficient spending. The essence of the much glorified "progressive" economic policies of the last decades was to expropriate ever-increasing parts of the higher incomes and to employ the funds thus raised for financing public waste and for subsidizing the members of the most powerful pressure groups. In the eyes of the "unorthodox," every kind of policy, however manifest its inadequacy may have been, was justified as a means of bringing about more equality. Now this process has reached its end. With the present tax rates and the methods applied in the control of prices, profits and interest rates, the system has liquidated itself. Even the confiscation of every penny earned above 1,000 pounds a year will not provide any perceptible increase to Great Britain's public revenue. The most bigoted Fabians cannot fail to realize that henceforth funds for public spending must be taken from the same people who are supposed to profit from it. Great Britain has reached the limit both of monetary expansionism and of spending.

Conditions in this country are not essentially different. The Keynesian recipe to make wage rates soar no longer works. Credit expansion, on an unprecedented scale engineered by the New Deal, for a short time delayed the consequences of inappropriate labor policies. During this interval the Administration and the union bosses could boast of the "social gains" they had secured for the "common man." But now the inevitable consequences of the increase in the quantity of money and deposits has become visible; prices are rising higher and higher. What is going on today in the United States is the final failure of Keynesianism.

There is no doubt that the American public is moving away from the Keynesian notions and slogans. Their prestige is dwindling. Only a few years ago politicians were naively discussing the extent of national income in dollars without taking into account the changes which government-made inflation had brought about in the dollar's purchasing power. Demagogues specified the level to which they wanted to bring the national (dollar) income. Today this form of reasoning is no longer popular. At last the "common man" has learned that increasing the quantity of dollars does not make America richer. Professor Harris still praises the Roosevelt Administration for having raised dollar incomes. But such Keynesian consistency is found today only in classrooms.

There are still teachers who tell their students that "an economy can lift itself by its own bootstraps" and that "we can spend our way into prosperity." * But the Keynesian miracle fails to materialize; the stones do not turn into bread. The panegyrics of the learned authors who cooperated in the production of the present volume merely confirm the editor's introductory statement that "Keynes could awaken in his disciples an almost religious fervor for his economics, which could be effectively harnessed for the dissemination of the new economics." And Professor Harris goes on to say, "Keynes indeed had the Revelation."

* Cf. Lorie Tarshis, *The Elements of Economics*, New York 1947, p. 565.

There is no use in arguing with people who are driven by "an almost religious fervor" and believe that their master "had the Revelation." It is one of the tasks of economics to analyze carefully each of the inflationist plans, those of Keynes and Gesell no less than those of their innumerable predecessors from John Law down to Major Douglas. Yet no one should expect that any logical argument or any experience could ever shake the almost religious fervor of those who believe in salvation through spending and credit expansion.

12

Liberty and Its Antithesis

As the harbingers of socialism tell us again and again, socialism will not only make all people rich, but will also bring perfect freedom to everybody. The transition to socialism, declares Frederick Engels, the friend and collaborator of Marx, is the leap of mankind from the realm of necessity into the realm of freedom. Under capitalism, say the Communists, there is bondage for the immense majority; in the Soviet Union alone there is genuine liberty for all.

The treatment of this problem of freedom and bondage has been muddled by confounding it with the issues of the nature-given conditions of man's existence. In nature there is nothing that could be called freedom. Nature is inexorable necessity. It is the state of affairs into which all created beings are placed and with which they have to cope. Man has to adjust his conduct to the world as it is. He lacks the power to rise in rebellion against the "laws of nature." If he wants to substitute more satisfactory conditions for less satisfactory, he has to comply with them.

Freedom in Society Means Freedom for Individuals to Choose

The concept of freedom and its antithesis make sense only in referring to the conditions of social cooperation among men. Social cooperation, the basis of any really human and civilized existence, can be achieved by two different methods. It can be cooperation by virtue of contract and voluntary coordination on the part of all individuals, or it can be cooperation by virtue of command on the part of a Führer and compulsory subordination of the many. The latter system is authoritarian.

In the libertarian system every individual is a moral person, that is, he is free to choose and to act and is responsible for his conduct. In the authoritarian system the supreme chief alone is a free agent while all the others are bondsmen subject to his discretion. Where the authoritarian system is fully established, as was for instance the case in the empire of the Inca in pre-Columbian America, the subjects are merely in a zoological sense human; virtually they are deprived of their specifically human faculty of choosing and acting and are not accountable for their conduct. It was in accordance with this degradation of man's moral dignity that the Nazi criminals declined any responsibility for their deeds by pointing out that all they did was to obey the orders of their superiors.

Western civilization is based upon the libertarian principle, and all its achievements are the result of the actions of free men. Only in the frame of a free society is it meaningful to distinguish between what is good and ought to be done and what is bad and ought to be avoided. Only in such a free society has the individual the power to choose between morally commendable and morally reprehensible conduct.

Man is not a perfect being and there is no perfection in human affairs. Conditions in the free society are certainly in many regards unsatisfactory. There is still ample room for the endeavors of those who are intent upon fighting evil and raising the moral, intellectual and material level of mankind.

Socialism Leads to Total Control

But the designs of the Communists, Socialists, and all their allies aim at something else. They want to establish the authoritarian system. What they mean in extolling the benefits to be derived from what they call "planning" is a society in which all of the people should be prevented from planning their own conduct and from arranging their lives according to their own moral convictions. One plan alone should prevail, the plan of the great idol State (with a capital S), the plan of the supreme chief of the government, enforced by the police. Every individual should be forced to renounce his autonomy and to obey, without asking questions, the orders issued from the Politburo, the Führer's secretariat. This is the kind of freedom that Engels had in mind. It is precisely the opposite of what the term freedom used to signify up to our age.

It was the great merit of Professor Friedrich von Hayek to have directed attention to the authoritarian character of the socialist schemes, whether they are advocated by international or by nationalist socialists, by atheists or by misguided believers, by white-skinned or by dark-skinned fanatics. Although there have always been authors who exposed the authoritarianism of the socialist designs, the main criticism of socialism centered around its economic inadequacy, and did not sufficiently deal with its effects upon the lives of the citizens. Because of this neglect of the human angle of the issue, the great majority of those supporting socialist policies vaguely assumed that the restriction of the individuals' freedom by a socialist regime will apply "only" to economic matters and will not affect freedom in non-economic affairs.

But as Hayek in 1944 clearly pointed out in his book *The Road To Serfdom*, economic control is not merely control of a sector of human life that can be separated from the rest; it is the control of the means for all our ends. As the socialist state has sole control of the means, it has the power to determine which ends are to be served and what men are to strive for. It is not an accident that Marxian socialism in Russia and nationalist socialism in Germany resulted in the complete abolition of all civil liberties and the establishment of the most rigid despotism. Tyranny is the political corollary of socialism, as representative government is the political corollary of the market economy.

Now Professor Hayek has enlarged and substantiated his ideas in a comprehensive treatise, *The Constitution of Liberty*.* In the first two parts of this book the author provides a brilliant exposition of the meaning of liberty and the creative powers of a free civilization. Endorsing the famous definition that describes liberty as the rule of laws and not of men, he analyzes the constitutional and legal foundations of a commonwealth of free citizens. He contrasts the two schemes of society's social and political organization, government by the people (representative government) based upon legality, and government by the discretionary power of an authoritarian ruler or a ruling clique, an *Obrigkeit* as the Germans used to call it. Fully appreciating the moral, practical and material superiority of the former, he shows in detail what the legal requirements of such a state of affairs are and what has to be done in order to make it work and to defend it against the machinations of its foes.

---

* F. A. Hayek, *The Constitution of Liberty*, the University of Chicago Press, 1959, 580 pages.

The Welfare State Leads to Socialism

Unfortunately, the third part of Professor Hayek's book is rather disappointing. Here the author tries to distinguish between socialism and the Welfare State. Socialism, he alleges, is on the decline; the Welfare State is supplanting it. And he thinks that the Welfare State is, under certain conditions, compatible with liberty.

In fact, the Welfare State is merely a method for transforming the market economy step by step into socialism. The original plan of socialist action as developed by Karl Marx in 1848 in the *Communist Manifesto* aimed at a gradual realization of socialism by a series of governmental measures. The ten most powerful of such measures were enumerated in the *Manifesto*. They are well known to everybody because they are the very measures that form the essence of the activities of the Welfare State, of Bismarck's and the kaiser's German *Sozialpolitik* as well as of the American New Deal and British Fabian Socialism. The *Communist Manifesto* calls these measures which it suggests "economically insufficient and untenable," but it stresses the fact that "in the course of the movement [they] outstrip themselves, necessitate further inroads upon the old social order, and are unavoidable as a means of entirely revolutionizing the mode of production."

Later, Marx adopted a different method for the policies of his party. He abandoned the tactics of a gradual approach to the total state of socialism and instead advocated a violent revolutionary overthrow of the "bourgeois" system that at one stroke should "liquidate" the "exploiters" and establish "the dictatorship of the proletariat." It was this that Lenin did in 1917 in Russia and what the Communist International plans to achieve everywhere. What separates the Communists from the advocates of the Welfare State is not the ultimate goal of their endeavors, but the methods by means of which they want to attain a goal that is common to both of them. The difference of opinions that divides them is the same that distinguishes the Marx of 1848 from the Marx of 1867, the year of the first publication of the first volume of *Das Kapital*.

The Failure of Economic Planning

However, the fact that Professor Hayek has misjudged the character of the Welfare State does not seriously detract from the value of his great book. For his searching analysis of the policies and concerns of the Welfare State shows to every thoughtful reader why and how these much-praised welfare policies inevitably always fail. These policies never attain those—allegedly beneficial—ends which the government and the self-styled progressives who advocated them wanted to attain, but—on the contrary—bring about a state of affairs which—from the very point of view of the government and its supporters—is even more unsatisfactory than the previous state of affairs they wanted to "improve." If the government does not repeal its first intervention, it is induced to supplement it by further acts of intervention. As these fail again, still more meddling with business is resorted to until all economic freedom has been virtually abolished. What emerges is the system of all-round planning, i.e., socialism of the type which the German Hindenburg Plan was aiming at in the First World War and which was later put into effect by Hitler after his seizure of power, and by the British Coalition Cabinet in the Second World War.

The main error that prevents many of our contemporaries from adequately comprehending the significance of various party programs and the trend of the welfare policies is their failure to recognize that there is apart from outright nationalization of all plants and farms (as effected in Russia and China) a second method for the full realization of socialism. Under this system that is commonly called "planning" (or, in war time, war socialism) the various plants and farms remain outwardly and seemingly units, but they become entirely and unconditionally subject to the orders of the supreme planning authority. Every citizen, whatever his nominal position in the economic system may be, is bound to toil in strict compliance with the orders of the planning board, and his income—the amount he is permitted to spend for his consumption—is exclusively determined by these orders. Some labels and terms of the capitalistic system may be preserved, but they signify under the altered conditions something entirely different from what they used to signify in the market economy. Other terms may be changed. Thus in Hitler Germany the head of an outfit who supplanted the entrepreneur or the corporation president of the market economy was styled "shop manager" (*Betriebsführer*) and the labor force "followers" (*Gefolgschaft*). As the theoretical pace-makers of this system, e.g., the late Professor Othmar Spann, has pointed out again and again, it retains only the name of private ownership, while in fact there is exclusively public—state—ownership.

Only by paying full attention to these fundamental issues can one form a correct appreciation of the political controversies in the nations of Western civilization. For if socialism and communism should succeed in these countries, it will be the socialism of the planning scheme and not the socialism of the nationalization scheme. The latter is a method applicable to predominantly agricultural countries like those of Eastern Europe and Asia. In the industrial countries of the West the planning scheme is more popular because even the most fanatical statolatrists shrink from directly nationalizing the intricate apparatus of modern manufacturing.

Yet the "planning scheme" is just as destructive of freedom as the "nationalization scheme" and both lead on to the authoritarian state.

CW **PART 4**

Ideas

Profit is a product of the mind, of success in anticipating the future state of the market. It is a spiritual and intellectual phenomenon. . . .

Men must choose between capitalism and socialism. They cannot avoid this dilemma by resorting to a capitalist system without entrepreneurial profit. . . . If control of production is shifted from the hands of entrepreneurs, daily anew elected by a plebiscite of the consumers, into the hands of the supreme commander . . . neither representative government nor any civil liberties can survive.

—"Profit and Loss"

13

My Contributions to Economic Theory

Your kind invitation to address you on my contributions to economic theory honors me greatly. It is not an easy task. Looking back on my work, I realize very well that the share of one individual in the total achievements of an epoch is small indeed, that he is indebted not only to his predecessors and teachers, but to all his colleagues and no less to his pupils. I know how much I owe to the economists of this country in particular since the time, many years ago, when my teacher Böhm-Bawerk directed my attention to the study of the works of John Bates Clark, Frank A. Fetter, and other American scholars. And during all my activities, the recognition of my contributions by American economists encouraged me. Nor can I forget that, when still a student at the University of Vienna, I published a monograph on the development of Austrian labor legislation, an American economist was the first who showed an interest in it. And later the first scholar who appreciated my *The Theory of Money and Credit* was again an American, my distinguished friend Professor B. M. Anderson, in his book *The Value of Money*, published in 1917.

Monetary Theory

When I first began to study the problems of monetary theory there was a general belief, namely, that modern marginal utility economics was unable to deal with monetary theory in a satisfactory way. Helfferich was the most outspoken of those who held this opinion. In his *Treatise on Money* he tried to establish that marginal utility analysis must necessarily fail in its attempts to build up a theory of money.

Address delivered before the economics faculty of New York University at the Faculty Club on November 20, 1940.

This challenge provided me with the incentive to use the methods of modern marginal utility economics in the study of monetary problems. To do so I had to use an approach radically different from that of the mathematical economists who try to establish the formulas of the so-called equation of exchange.

In dealing with such an equation the mathematical economist assumes that something (obviously, one of the elements of the equation) changes and that corresponding changes in the other values must needs follow. These elements of the equation are not items in the individual's economy, but categories of the whole economic system, and consequently the changes do not occur with individuals but with the whole system, with the *Volkswirtschaft* as a whole. This way of reasoning is eminently unrealistic and differs radically from the procedure of modern catallactics.* It is a return to the manner of reasoning which doomed to frustration the work of the older Classical economists. Monetary problems are economic problems and have to be dealt with in the same way as all other economic problems. The monetary economist does not have to deal with universal entities like volume of trade meaning total volume of trade, or quantity of money meaning all the money current in the whole economic system. Still less can he make use of the nebulous metaphor "velocity of circulation." He has to realize that the demand for money arises from the preferences of individuals within a market society. Because everybody wishes to have a certain amount of cash, sometimes more, sometimes less, there is a demand for money. Money is never simply in the economic system, money is never simply circulating. All the money available is always in the cash-holdings of somebody. Every piece of money may one day—sometimes oftener, sometimes more seldom—pass from one man's cash-holding to another man's. But at every moment it is owned by somebody and is a part of somebody's cash-holdings. The decisions of individuals regarding the magnitude of their cash-holding, their choices between the disutility of holding more cash and its advantages constitute the ultimate factor in the formation of purchasing power.

---

* Catallactics is a name for the science of exchanges, the "branch of knowledge to investigate the market phenomena, that is, the determination of the mutual exchange ratios of the goods and services negotiated on markets, their origin in human action and their effects upon later action." Mises, *Human Action* [1966, 1996, and Liberty Fund, 2007], page 232.

Changes in the supply of money or in the demand for it can never occur for all individuals at the same time and to the same extent and they, therefore, never affect their judgments of value and their behavior as buyers and sellers to the same degree. Therefore the changes in prices do not affect all commodities at the same time and to the same degree. The over-simple formula both of the primitive quantity theory and of contemporary mathematical economists according to which prices, that is, all prices, rise or fall in the proportion of the increase or decrease in the quantity of money is absolutely wrong.

We have to study monetary changes as changes which occur first for some groups of individuals only and slowly spread over the whole economic system to the extent that the additional demand of those first benefited reaches other classes of individuals. Only in this way can we obtain a realistic insight into the social consequences of monetary changes.

The Business Cycle

Taking this as my point of departure I developed a general theory of money and credit and tried to explain the business cycle as a credit phenomenon. This theory, which is today styled the monetary theory or sometimes the Austrian theory of the trade cycle, led me to make some criticism of the continental, especially of the German, credit system. Readers were at first more interested in my pessimistic judgment of the trends of German Central Bank policy and my pessimistic forecast which nobody believed in 1912 until a few years later things turned out much worse even than I had predicted. It is the fate of the economist that people are more interested in his conclusions than in his explanations, and that they are reluctant to abandon a policy whose undesired but inevitable results the economist has demonstrated.

Economic Calculation under Socialism

From my studies of monetary and credit problems, which later stimulated me to found the Austrian Institute of Business Cycle Research, I came to the study of the problem of economic calculation within a socialist community. In my essay on economic calculation in a socialist world, first published in 1920, and then later in my book on *Socialism*, I

have proved that an economic system, where there is no private ownership of the means of production, could not find any criterion for determining the values of the factors of production and therefore could not
calculate. Since I first touched upon this point, many dozens of books
and many hundreds of articles published in different languages have
dealt with the problem; this discussion has left my thesis unshattered.
The treatment of the problems connected with planning, of course total planning and socialization, has been given a completely new direction by the indication of this as the crucial point.

Is There a Middle Way?

From the comparative study of the essential features both of capitalist
and socialist economy I came to the related problem of whether, apart
from these two thinkable systems of social cooperation, i.e., private
ownership of the means of production and public ownership, there is
a third possible social system. Such a third solution, a system which
its proponents claim is neither socialism nor capitalism, but midway
between both and avoiding the disadvantages of each and retaining
the advantages of both, has again and again been suggested. I tried to
examine the economic implications of these systems of government
interference and to demonstrate that they can never attain the ends
which people wish to attain with them. I later broadened the field of
my research in order to include the problems of the *stato corporativo*,
the panacea recommended by fascism.

Human Action

Occupation with all these problems made necessary an approach to
the question of the values and ends of human activity. The reproach of
sociologists to the effect that economists deal only with an unrealistic
"economic man" could no longer be endured. I tried to demonstrate
that the economists were never so narrow as their critics believed. The
prices whose formation we try to explain are a function of demand and
it does not make any difference what kind of motives actuated those involved in the transaction. It is immaterial whether the motives of those
who wish to buy are egoistic or altruistic, moral or immoral, patriotic or
unpatriotic. Economics deals with the scarce means of attaining ends,
irrespective of the quality of the ends. The ends are beyond the scope

of rationality, but every action of a conscious being directed towards a specific goal is necessarily rational. It is futile to convict economics because it is rational and deals with rationality. Of course, science is always rational.

In my treatise on economic theory,* published in the German language in Geneva a few months ago—an English edition will be published in the near future†—I have dealt not only with the economic problems of a market society but in the same way with the economics of all other thinkable types of social cooperation. I think that this is indispensable in a world where the fundamental principles of economic organization are at stake.

I try in my treatise to consider the concept of static equilibrium as instrumental only and to make use of this purely hypothetical abstraction only as a means of approaching an understanding of a continuously changing world. It is one of the shortcomings of many economic theorists that they have forgotten the purpose underlying the introduction of this hypothetical concept into our analysis. We cannot do without this notion of a world where there is no change; but we have to use it only for the purpose of studying changes and their consequences, that means for the study of risk and uncertainty and therefore of profits and losses.

Capital Accumulation and Interest Theory

The logical result of this view is the disintegration of some mythical interpretations of economic entities. The almost metaphysical use of terms like capital has to be avoided. There is in nature nothing which corresponds to the terms capital or income. There are different commodities, producers goods, and consumers goods; it is the intention of the individuals or of acting groups which makes some goods capital and others income. The maintenance of capital or the accumulation of new capital is always the outcome of a conscious action on the part of men who restrict their consumption to limits which do not reduce the value of the stock available. It is a mistake to assume the immuta-

---

* *Nationalökonomie, Theorie des Handelns und Wirtschaftens*, Éditions Union, Geneva, Switzerland, May 1940, 772 pages.
† [Editor's note: Mises's *Human Action*, first published by Yale University Press in 1949, was a complete rewrite, not a translation, of his 1940 *Nationaloekonomie*.]

bility of the capital stock as something natural which does not require special attention. In this respect I have to disagree with the opinions of one of the most eminent economists of our time, with Professor Knight of Chicago.

The weak point of the Böhm-Bawerkian theory [of capital and interest] is not, as Professor Knight believes, the useless introduction of the concept of the period of production. It is a more serious deficiency that Böhm-Bawerk reverts to the errors of the so-called productivity theory. Like Professor Fetter of Princeton I aimed at an elimination of this weakness by basing the explanation of interest on time preference only.

The touchstone of any economic theory is according to an oft-quoted dictum, the treatment of the trade cycle. I have tried not only to restate the monetary theory of the cycle but also to demonstrate that all other explanations cannot avoid using the main argument of this theory. Of course, the boom means an upward movement of prices or at least a compensation for tendencies working toward falling prices, and to explain this requires the postulation of a rising supply of credit or money.

Economist's Role: Challenge Economic Error

In every part of my treatise I try to take into account the relative weight to be assigned to different institutional factors and to different economic data. I further discuss the objections raised not only by different theoretical schools but also by those who deny the possibility of any economic science. The economist has to answer those who believe that there is no such thing as a universally valid science of society, who doubt the unity of human logic and experience and try to replace what they call international and, therefore, as they say, vain knowledge with doctrines which represent the peculiar point of view of their own class, nation or race. We do not have the right to let these pretensions pass unchallenged even if we have to assert truths which to us seem obvious. But it is sometimes necessary to repeat truths because we find repeated instances of the old errors.

14

Economic Teaching at the Universities

A few years ago a House of Representatives subcommittee on publicity and propaganda in the executive departments, under the chairmanship of Representative Forest A. Harness, investigated federal propaganda operations. On one occasion the committee had as a witness a government-employed doctor. When asked if his public speeches throughout the country presented both sides of the discussion touching compulsory national health insurance, this witness answered: "I don't know what you mean by both sides."

This naive answer throws light on the state of mind of people who proudly call themselves progressive intellectuals. They simply do not imagine that any argument could be advanced against the various schemes they are suggesting. As they see it, everybody, without asking questions, must support every project aiming at more and more government control of all aspects of the citizen's life and conduct. They never try to refute the objections raised against their doctrines. They prefer, as Mrs. Eleanor Roosevelt recently did in her column, to call dishonest those with whom they do not agree.

Many eminent citizens hold educational institutions responsible for the spread of this bigotry. They sharply criticize the way in which economics, philosophy, sociology, history and political science are taught at most American universities and colleges. They blame many teachers for indoctrinating their students with the ideas of all-round planning, socialism and communism. Some of those attacked try to deny any responsibility. Others, realizing the futility of this mode of defense, cry out about "persecution" and infringement of "academic freedom."

Originally published in *The Freeman*, April 7, 1952, as "Our Leftist Economic Teaching." Reprinted with permission from the Foundation for Economic Education.

Yet what is unsatisfactory with present-day academic conditions—not only in this country but in most foreign nations—is not the fact that many teachers are blindly committed to Veblenian, Marxian and Keynesian fallacies, and try to convince their students that no tenable objections can be raised against what they call progressive policies. The mischief is rather to be seen in the fact that the statements of these teachers are not challenged by any criticism in the academic sphere. The pseudo-liberals monopolize the teaching jobs at many universities. Only men who agree with them are appointed as teachers and instructors of the social sciences, and only textbooks supporting their ideas are used. The essential question is not how to get rid of inept teachers and poor textbooks. It is how to give the students an opportunity to hear something about the ideas of economists rejecting the tenets of the interventionists, inflationists, Socialists and Communists.

Methods of the "Progressive" Teachers

Let us illustrate the matter by reviewing a recently published book. A professor of Harvard University edits, with the support of an advisory committee whose members are all like himself professors of economics at Harvard University, a series of textbooks, the "Economics Handbook Series." In this series there was published a volume on socialism. Its author, Paul M. Sweezy, opens his preface with the declaration that the book "is written from the standpoint of a Socialist." The editor of the series, Professor Seymour E. Harris, in his introduction goes a step further in stating that the author's "viewpoint is nearer that of the group which determines Soviet policy than the one which now [1949] holds the reins of government in Britain." This is a mild description of the fact that the volume is from the first to the last page an uncritical eulogy of the Soviet system.

Now it is perfectly legitimate for Dr. Sweezy to write such a book and for professors to edit and to publish it. The United States is a free country—one of the few free countries left in the world—and the Constitution and its amendments grant to everybody the right to think as he likes and to have published in print what he thinks. Sweezy has in fact unwittingly rendered a great service to the discerning public. For his volume clearly shows to every judicious reader conversant with economics that the most eminent advocates of socialism are at their wits' end, do not know how to advance any plausible argument in favor of their creed, and are utterly at a loss to refute any of the serious objections raised against it.

But the book is not designed for perspicacious scholars well acquainted with the social sciences. It is, as the editors' introduction emphasizes, written for the general reader in order to popularize ideas and especially also for use in the classroom. Laymen and students who know nothing or very little about the problems involved will draw all their knowledge about socialism from it. They lack the familiarity with theories and facts which would enable them to form an independent opinion about the various doctrines expounded by the author. They will accept all his theses and descriptions as incontestable science and wisdom. How could they be so presumptuous as to doubt the reliability of a book, written, as the introduction says, by an "authority" in the field and sponsored by a committee of professors of venerable Harvard!

The shortcoming of the committee is not to be seen in the fact that they have published such a book, but in the fact that their series contains only this book about socialism. If they had, together with Dr. Sweezy's book, published another volume critically analyzing communist ideas and the achievements of socialist governments, nobody could blame them for disseminating communism. Decency should have impelled them to give the critics of socialism and communism the same chance to represent their views to the students of universities and colleges as they gave to Dr. Sweezy.

On every page of Dr. Sweezy's book one finds really amazing statements. Thus, in dealing with the problem of civil rights under a socialist regime, he simply equates the Soviet Constitution with the American Constitution. Both, he declares, are

generally accepted as the statement of the ideals which ought to guide the actions of both the state and the individual citizen. That these ideals are not always lived up to—either in the Soviet Union or in the United States—is certainly both true and important; but it does not mean that they do not exist or that they can be ignored, still less that they can be transformed into their opposite.

Leaving aside most of what could be advanced to explode this reasoning, there is need to realize that the American Constitution is not merely an ideal but the valid law of the country. To prevent it from becoming a dead letter there is an independent judiciary culminating in the Supreme Court. Without such a guardian of law and legality any law can be and is ignored and transformed into its opposite. Did Dr. Sweezy never become aware of this nuance? Does he really believe that the millions languishing in Soviet prisons and labor camps can invoke habeas corpus?

To say it again: Dr. Sweezy has the right—precisely because the American Bill of Rights is not merely an ideal, but an enforced law—to transform every fact into its opposite. But professors who hand out such praise of the Soviets to their students without informing them about the opinions of the opponents of socialism must not raise the cry of witchhunt if they are criticized.

Professor Harris in his introduction contends that "those who fear undue influence of the present volume may be cheered by a forthcoming companion volume on capitalism in this series written by one as devoted to private enterprise as Dr. Sweezy is to socialism." This volume, written by Professor David McCord Wright of the University of Virginia, has been published in the meantime. It deals incidentally also with socialism and tries to explode some minor socialist fallacies, such as the doctrine of the withering away of the State, a doctrine which even the most fanatical Soviet authors relegate today to an insignificant position. But it certainly cannot be considered a satisfactory substitute, or a substitute at all, for a thoroughly critical examination of the whole body of socialist and communist ideas and the lamentable failure of all socialist experiments.

Some of the teachers try to refute the accusations of ideological intolerance leveled against their universities and to demonstrate their own impartiality by occasionally inviting a dissenting outsider to address their students. This is mere eyewash. One hour of sound economics against several years of indoctrination of errors! The present writer may quote from a letter in which he declined such an invitation:

> What makes it impossible for me to present the operation of the market economy in a short lecture—whether fifty minutes or twice fifty minutes—is the fact that people, influenced by the prevailing ideas on economic problems, are full of erroneous opinions concerning this system. They are convinced that economic depressions, mass unemployment, monopoly, aggressive imperialism and wars, and the poverty of the greater part of mankind, are caused by the unhampered operation of the capitalist mode of production.
>
> If a lecturer does not dispel each of these dogmas, the impression left with the audience is unsatisfactory. Now, exploding any one of them re-

quires much more time than that assigned to me in your program. The hearers will think: "He did not refer at all to this" or "He made only a few casual remarks about that." My lecture would rather confirm them in their misunderstanding of the system. . . . If it were possible to expound the operation of capitalism in one or two short addresses, it would be a waste of time to keep the students of economics for several years at the universities. It would be difficult to explain why voluminous textbooks have to be written about this subject. . . . It is these reasons that impel me reluctantly to decline your kind invitation.

The Alleged Impartiality of the Universities

The pseudo-progressive teachers excuse their policy of barring all those whom they smear as old-fashioned reactionaries from access to teaching positions by calling these men biased.

The reference to bias is quite out of place if the accuser is not in a position to demonstrate clearly in what the deficiency of the smeared author's doctrine consists. The only thing that matters is whether a doctrine is sound or unsound. This is to be established by facts and deductive reasoning. If no tenable arguments can be advanced to invalidate a theory, it does not in the least detract from its correctness if the author is called names. If, on the other hand, the falsity of a doctrine has already been clearly demonstrated by an irrefutable chain of reasoning, there is no need to call its author biased.

A biographer may try to explain the manifestly exploded errors of the person whose life he is writing about by tracing them back to bias. But such psychological interpretation is immaterial in discussions concerning the correctness or falsity of a theory. Professors who call those with whom they disagree biased merely confess their inability to discover any fault in their adversaries' theories.

Many "progressive" professors have for some time served in one of the various alphabetical government agencies. The tasks entrusted to them in the bureaus were as a rule ancillary only. They compiled statistics and wrote memoranda which their superiors, either politicians or former managers of corporations, filed without reading. The professors did not instill a scientific spirit into the bureaus. But the bureaus gave them the mentality of authoritarianism. They distrust the populace and consider the State (with a capital S) as the God-sent guardian of the wretched underlings. Only the Government is impartial and unbiased. Whoever opposes any expansion of governmental powers is by this token unmasked as an enemy of the commonweal. It is manifest that he "hates" the State.

Now if an economist is opposed to the socialization of industries, he does not "hate" the State. He simply declares that the commonwealth is better served by private ownership of the means of production than by public ownership. Nobody could pretend that experience with nationalized enterprises contradicts this opinion.

Another typically bureaucratic prejudice which the professors acquired in Washington is to call the attitudes of those opposing government controls and the establishment of new offices "negativism." In the light of this terminology all that has been achieved by the American individual enterprise system is only "negative"; the bureaus alone are "positive."

There is, furthermore, the spurious antithesis "plan or no plan." Only totalitarian government planning that reduces the citizens to mere pawns in the designs of the bureaucracy is called planning. The plans of the individual citizens are simply "no plans." What semantics!

How Modern History Is Taught

The progressive intellectual looks upon capitalism as the most ghastly of all evils. Mankind, he contends, lived rather happily in the good old days. But then, as a British historian said, the Industrial Revolution "fell like a war or a plague" on the peoples. The "bourgeoisie" converted plenty into scarcity. A few tycoons enjoy all luxuries. But, as Marx himself observed, the worker "sinks deeper and deeper" because the bourgeoisie "is incompetent to assure an existence to its slave within his slavery."

Still worse are the intellectual and moral effects of the capitalist mode of production. There is but one means, the progressive believes, to free mankind from the misery and degradation produced by laissez-faire and rugged individualism, viz., to adopt central planning, the system with which the Russians are successfully experimenting. It is true that the results obtained by the Soviets are not yet fully satisfactory. But these shortcomings were caused only by the peculiar conditions of Russia. The West will avoid the pitfalls of the Russians and will realize the Welfare State without the merely accidental features that disfigured it in Russia and in Hitler Germany.

Such is the philosophy taught at most present-day schools and propagated by novels and plays. It is this doctrine that guides the actions of almost all contemporary governments. The American "progressive" feels ashamed of what he calls the social backwardness of his country. He considers it a duty of the United States to subsidize foreign socialist governments lavishly in order to enable them to go on with their ruinous socialist ventures. In his eyes the real enemy of the American people is Big Business, that is, the enterprises which provide the American common man with the highest standard of living ever reached in history. He hails every step forward on the road toward all-round control of business as progress. He smears all those who hint at the pernicious effects of waste, deficit spending and capital decumulation as reactionaries, economic royalists and Fascists. He never mentions the new or improved products which business almost every year makes accessible to the masses. But he goes into raptures about the rather questionable achievements of the Tennessee Valley Authority, the deficit of which is made good out of taxes collected from Big Business.

The most infatuated expositors of this ideology are to be found in the university departments of history, political science, sociology and literature. The professors of these departments enjoy the advantage, in referring to economic issues, that they are talking about a subject with which they are not familiar at all. This is especially flagrant in the case of historians. The way in which the history of the last two hundred years has been treated is really a scandal. Only recently eminent scholars have begun to unmask the crude fallacies of Lujo Brentano, the Webbs, the Hammonds, Tawney, Arnold Toynbee, Elie Halévy, the Beards and other authors. At the last meeting of the Mont Pèlerin Society the occupant of the chair of economic history at the London School of Economics, Professor T. S. Ashton, presented a paper in which he pointed out that the commonly accepted views of the economic developments of the nineteenth century "are not informed by any glimmering of economic sense." The historians tortured the facts when they concocted the legend that "the dominant form of organization under industrial capitalism, the factory, arose out of the demands, not of ordinary people, but of the rich and the rulers."

The truth is that the characteristic feature of capitalism was and is mass production for the needs of the masses. Whenever the factory with its methods of mass production by means of power-driven machines invaded a new branch of production, it started with cheap goods for the broad masses. The factories turned to the production of more refined and therefore more expensive merchandise only at a later stage, when the unprecedented improvement which they had caused in the masses' standard of living made it reasonable to apply the methods of mass production to better articles as well. Big business caters to the needs of the many; it depends exclusively upon mass consumption. In his capacity as consumer the common man is the sovereign whose buying or abstention from buying decides the fate of entrepreneurial activities. The "proletarian" is the much-talked-about customer who is *always right*.

The most popular method of deprecating capitalism is to make it responsible for every condition which is considered unsatisfactory. Tuberculosis, and, until a few years ago, syphilis, were called diseases of capitalism. The destitution of scores of millions in countries like India, which did *not* adopt capitalism, is blamed on capitalism. It is a sad fact that people become debilitated in old age and finally die. But this happens not only to salesmen but also to employers, and it was no less tragic in the pre-capitalistic ages than it is under capitalism. Prostitution, dipsomania and drug addiction are all called capitalist vices.

Whenever people discuss the alleged misdeeds of the capitalists, a learned professor or a sophisticated artist refers to the high income of movie stars, boxers and wrestlers. But who contributes more to these incomes, the millionaires or the "proletarians"?

It must be admitted that the worst excesses in this propaganda are not committed by professors of economics but by the teachers of the other social sciences, by journalists, writers and sometimes even by ministers. But the source from which all the slogans of this hectic fanaticism spring is the teachings handed down by the "institutionalist" school of economic policies. All these dogmas and fallacies can be ultimately traced back to allegedly economic doctrines.

The Proscription of Sound Economics

The Marxians, Keynesians, Veblenians and other "progressives" know very well that their doctrines cannot stand any critical analysis. They are fully aware of the fact that one representative of sound economics in their department would nullify all their teachings. This is why they are so anxious to bar every "orthodox" from access to the strongholds of their "un-orthodoxy."

The worst consequence of this proscription of sound economics is the fact that gifted young graduates shun the career of an academic economist. They do not want to be boycotted by universities, book reviewers and publishing firms. They prefer to go into business or the practice of law, where their talents will be fairly appreciated. It is mainly compromisers, who are not eager to find out the shortcomings of the official doctrine, who aspire to the teaching positions. There are few competent men left to take the place of the eminent scholars who die or reach the retirement age. Among the rising generation of instructors are hardly any worthy successors of such economists as Frank A. Fetter and Edwin W. Kemmerer of Princeton, Irving Fisher of Yale and Benjamin M. Anderson of California.

There is but one way to remedy this situation. True economists must be given the same opportunity in our faculties which only the advocates of socialism and interventionism enjoy today. This is surely not too much to ask as long as this country has not yet gone totalitarian.

15

The Political Chances of
Genuine Liberalism

The outlook of many eminent champions of genuine liberalism is rather pessimistic today. As they see it, the vitriolic slogans of the socialists and interventionists call forth a better response from the masses than the cool reasoning of judicious men. The majority of the voters are just dull and mentally inert people who dislike thinking and are easily deceived by the enticing promises of irresponsible pied pipers. Subconscious inferiority complexes and envy push people toward the parties of the left. They rejoice in the policies of confiscating the greater part of the income and wealth of successful businessmen without grasping the fact that these policies harm their own material interests. Disregarding all the objections raised by economists, they firmly believe that they can get many good things for nothing. Even in the United States people, although enjoying the highest standard of living ever attained in history, are prepared to condemn capitalism as a vile economy of scarcity and to indulge in daydreams about an economy of abundance in which everybody will get everything "according to his needs." The case for freedom and material prosperity is hopeless. The future belongs to the demagogues who know nothing else than to dissipate the capital accumulated by previous generations. Mankind is plunging into a return to the dark ages. Western civilization is doomed.

The Ideas of the Masses Come from Intellectuals

The main error of this widespread pessimism is the belief that the destructionist ideas and policies of our age sprang from the proletarians and are a "revolt of the masses." In fact, the masses, precisely because

First printed in *Farmand*, February 17, 1951, Oslo, Norway.

they are not creative and do not develop philosophies of their own, follow the leaders. The ideologies which produced all the mischiefs and catastrophes of our century are not an achievement of the mob. They are the feat of pseudo-scholars and pseudo-intellectuals. They were propagated from the chairs of universities and from the pulpit, they were disseminated by the press, by novels and plays, and by the movies and the radio. The intellectuals converted the masses to socialism and interventionism. These ideologies owe the power they have today to the fact that all means of communication have been turned over to their supporters and almost all dissenters have been virtually silenced. What is needed to turn the flood is to change the mentality of the intellectuals. Then the masses will follow suit.

Furthermore it is not true that the ideas of genuine liberalism are too complicated to appeal to the untutored mind of the average voter. It is not a hopeless task to explain to the wage earners that the only means to raise wage rates *for all those eager to find jobs and to earn wages* is to increase the per head quota of capital invested. The pessimists underrate the mental abilities of the "common man" when they assert that he cannot grasp the disastrous consequences of policies resulting in capital decumulation. Why do all "underdeveloped countries" ask for American aid and American capital? Why do they not rather expect aid from socialist Russia?

Government Programs Raise Prices

The acme of the policies of all self-styled progressive parties and governments is to raise artificially the prices of vital commodities above the height they would have attained on the markets of unhampered laissez-faire capitalism. Only an infinitesimal fraction of the American people is interested in the preservation of a high price for sugar. The immense majority of the American voters are buyers and consumers, not producers and sellers of sugar. Nonetheless the American government is firmly committed to a policy of high sugar prices by rigorously restricting both the importation of sugar from abroad and domestic production. Similar policies are adopted with regard to the prices of bread, meat, butter, eggs, potatoes, cotton and many other agricultural products. It is a serious blunder to call this procedure indiscriminately a pro-farmers policy. Less than one fifth of the United States's total population are dependent upon agriculture for a living. Yet the interests of these people with regard to the prices of various agricultural products are not identical. The dairyman is not interested in a high, but in a low price for wheat, fodder, sugar and cotton. The owners of chicken farms are hurt by high prices of any agricultural product but chickens and eggs. It is obvious that the growers of cotton, grapes, oranges, apples, grapefruit and cranberries are prejudiced by a system which raises the prices of staple foods. Most of the items of the so-called pro-farm policy favor only a minority of the total farming population at the expense of the majority not only of the non-farming, but also of the farming population.

Things are hardly different in other fields. When the railroadmen or the workers of the building trades, supported by laws and administrative practices which are admittedly loaded against their employers, indulge in feather-bedding and other devices allegedly destined to "create more jobs," they are unfairly fleecing the immense majority of their fellow citizens. The unions of the printers enhance the prices of books and periodicals and thus affect all people eager to read and to learn. The so-called pro-labor policies bring about a state of affairs under which each group of wage earners is intent upon improving their own conditions at the expense of the consumers, viz., the enormous majority.

Nobody knows today whether he wins more from those policies which are favoring the group to which he himself belongs than he loses on account of the policies which favor all the other groups. But it is certain that all are adversely affected by the general drop in the productivity of industrial effort and output which these allegedly beneficial policies inevitably bring about.

Until a few years ago the advocates of these unsuitable policies tried to defend them by pointing out that their incidence reduces only the wealth and income of the rich and benefits the masses at the sole expense of useless parasites. There is no need to explode the fallacies of this reasoning. Even if we admit its conclusiveness for the sake of argument, we must realize that, with the exception of a few countries, this "surplus" fund of the rich has already been exhausted. Even Mr. Hugh Gaitskell, Sir Stafford Cripps's successor as the *Führer* of Great Britain's economy, could not help declaring that "there is not enough money to take away from England's rich to raise standards of living any further." In the United States the policy of "soaking the rich" has not yet gone so far as that. But if the trend of American politics is not entirely reversed very soon, this richest of all countries will have to face the same situation in a few years.

Prospects for a Genuine Liberal Revival

Conditions being such, the prospects for a genuinely liberal revival may appear propitious. At least fifty per cent of the voters are women, most of them housewives or prospective housewives. To the common sense of these women a program of low prices will make a strong appeal. They will certainly cast their ballot for candidates who proclaim: Do away peremptorily with all policies and measures destined to enhance prices above the height of the unhampered market! Do away with all this dismal stuff of price supports, parity prices, tariffs and quotas, intergovernmental commodity control agreements and so on! Abstain from increasing the quantity of money in circulation and from credit expansion, from all illusory attempts to lower the rate of interest and from deficit spending! What we want is low prices.

In the end these judicious householders will even succeed in convincing their husbands.

In the *Communist Manifesto* Karl Marx and Frederick Engels asserted: "The cheap prices of its commodities are the heavy artillery with which capitalism batters down all Chinese walls." We may hope that these cheap prices will also batter down the highest of all Chinese walls, viz., those erected by the folly of bad economic policies.

To express such hopes is not merely wishful thinking.

16

Trends Can Change

One of the cherished dogmas implied in contemporary fashionable doctrines is the belief that tendencies of social evolution as manifested in the recent past will prevail in the future too. Study of the past, it is assumed, discloses the shape of things to come. Any attempt to reverse or even to stop a trend is doomed to failure. Man must submit to the irresistible power of historical destiny.

To this dogma is added the Hegelian idea of progressive improvement in human conditions. Every later stage of history, Hegel taught, is of necessity a higher and more perfect state than the preceding one, is progress toward the ultimate goal which God in his infinite goodness set for mankind. Thus any doubt with regard to the excellence of what is bound to come is unwarranted, unscientific and blasphemous. Those fighting "progress" are not only committed to a hopeless venture. They are also morally wicked, *reactionary*, for they want to prevent the emergence of conditions that will benefit the immense majority.

From the point of view of this philosophy its adepts, the self-styled "progressives," deal with the fundamental issues of economic policies. They do not examine the merits and demerits of suggested measures and reforms. This would, in their eyes, be unscientific. As they see it, the only question that has to be answered is whether such proposed innovations do or do not agree with the spirit of our age and follow the direction which destiny has ordained for the course of human affairs. The drift of the policies of the recent past teaches us what is both inescapable and beneficial. The only legitimate source for the cognition of what is salutary and has to be accomplished today is the knowledge of what was accomplished yesterday.

Originally published in *The Freeman*, February 12, 1951. Reprinted with permission from the Foundation for Economic Education.

In the last decades there prevailed a trend toward more and more government interference with business. The sphere of the private citizen's initiative was narrowed down. Laws and administrative decrees restricted the field in which entrepreneurs and capitalists were free to conduct their activities in compliance with the wishes of the consumers as manifested in the structure of the market. From year to year an ever-increasing portion of profits and interest on capital invested was confiscated by taxation of corporation earnings and individual incomes and estates. "Social" control, i.e., government control, of business is step by step substituted for private control. The "progressives" are certain that this trend toward wresting "economic" power from the parasitic "leisure class" and its transfer to "the people" will go on until the "welfare state" will have supplanted the nefarious capitalistic system which history has doomed for ever. Notwithstanding sinister machinations on the part of "the interests," mankind, led by government economists and other bureaucrats, politicians, and union bosses, marches steadily toward the bliss of an earthly paradise.

The prestige of this myth is so enormous that it quells any opposition. It spreads defeatism among those who do not share the opinion that everything which comes later is better than what preceded and are fully aware of the disastrous effects of all-round planning, i.e., totalitarian socialism. They, too, meekly submit to what, the pseudo-scholars tell them, is inevitable. It is this mentality of passively accepting defeat that has made socialism triumph in many European countries and may very soon make it conquer in this country too.

The Marxian dogma of the inevitability of socialism was based on the thesis that capitalism necessarily results in progressive impoverishment of the immense majority of people. All the advantages of technological progress benefit exclusively the small minority of exploiters. The masses are condemned to increasing "misery, oppression, slavery, degradation, exploitation." No action on the part of governments or labor unions can succeed in stopping this evolution. Only socialism, which is bound to come "with the inexorability of a law of nature," will bring salvation by "the expropriation of the few usurpers by the mass of people."

Facts have belied this prognosis no less than all other Marxian forecasts. In the capitalist countries the common man's standard of living is today incomparably higher than it was in the days of Marx. It is simply not true that the fruits of technological improvement are enjoyed exclusively by the capitalists while the laborer, as the *Communist Manifesto* says, "instead of rising with the progress of industry, sinks deeper and deeper." Not a minority of "rugged individualists," but the masses, are the main consumers of the products turned out by large-scale production. Only morons can still cling to the fable that capitalism "is incompetent to assure an existence to its slave within his slavery."

Today the doctrine of the irreversibility of prevailing trends has supplanted the Marxian doctrine concerning the inevitability of progressive impoverishment.

Now this doctrine is devoid of any logical or experimental verification. Historical trends do not necessarily go on for ever. No practical man is so foolish as to assume that prices will keep rising because the price curves of the past show an upward tendency. On the contrary, the more prices soar, the more alarmed cautious businessmen become about a possible reversal. Almost all prognostications which our government statisticians made on the basis of their study of the figures available—which necessarily always refer to the past—have proved faulty. What is called extrapolation of trend lines is viewed by sound statistical theory with the utmost suspicion.

The same refers also to developments in fields which are not open to description by statistical figures. There was, for instance, in the course of ancient Greco-Roman civilization a tendency toward an interregional division of labor. The trade between the various parts of the vast Roman Empire intensified more and more. But then came a turning point. Commerce declined and there finally emerged the medieval manor system, with almost complete autarky of every landowner's household.

Or, to quote another example, there prevailed in the eighteenth century a tendency toward reducing the severity and the horrors of war. In 1770 the Comte de Guibert could write: "Today the whole of Europe is civilized. Wars have become less cruel. Except in combat no blood is shed; prisoners are respected; towns are no longer destroyed; the country is no more ravaged."

Can anybody maintain that this trend has not been changed?

But even if it were true that an historical trend must go on forever, and that therefore the coming of socialism is inevitable, it would still not be permissible to infer that socialism will be a better, or even more than that, the most perfect state of society's economic organization. There is nothing to support such a conclusion other than the arbitrary pseudo-theological surmises of Hegel, Comte and Marx, according to which every later stage of the historical process must necessarily be a better state. It is not true that human conditions must always improve, and that a relapse into very unsatisfactory modes of life, penury and barbarism is impossible. The comparatively high standard of living which the common man enjoys today in the capitalist countries is an achievement of laissez-faire capitalism. Neither theoretical reasoning nor historical experience allows the inference that it could be preserved, still less be improved under socialism.

In the last decades in many countries the number of divorces and of suicides has increased from year to year. Yet hardly anybody will have the temerity to contend that this trend means progress toward more satisfactory conditions.

The typical graduate of colleges and high schools very soon forgets most of the things he has learned. But there is one piece of indoctrination which makes a lasting impression on his mind, viz., the dogma of the irreversibility of the trend toward all-round planning and regimentation. He does not doubt the thesis that mankind will never return to capitalism, the dismal system of an age gone forever, and that the "wave of the future" carries us toward the promised land of Cockaigne. If he had any doubts, what he reads in newspapers and what he hears from the politicians would dispel them. For even the candidates nominated by the parties of opposition, although critical of the measures of the party in power, protest that they are not "reactionary," and do not venture to stop the march toward "progress."

Thus the average man is predisposed in favor of socialism. Of course, he does not approve of everything that the Soviets have done. He thinks that the Russians have blundered in many respects, and he excuses these errors as being caused by their unfamiliarity with freedom. He blames the leaders, especially Stalin, for the corruption of the lofty ideal of all-round planning. His sympathies go rather to Tito, the upright rebel, who refuses to surrender to Russia. Not so long ago he displayed the same friendly feelings for Benes, and until only a few months ago for Mao Tse-tung, the "agrarian reformer."

At any rate, a good part of American public opinion believes that this country is in essential matters backward, as it has not yet, like the Russians, wiped out production for profit and unemployment and has not yet attained stability. Practically nobody thinks that he could learn something important about these problems from a serious occupation with economics. The dogmas of the irreversibility of prevailing tendencies and of their unfailingly beneficial effects render such studies supererogatory. If economics confirms these dogmas, it is superfluous; if it is at variance with them, it is illusory and deceptive.

Now trends of evolution can change, and hitherto they almost always have changed. But they changed only because they met firm opposition. The prevailing trend toward what Hilaire Belloc called the servile state will certainly not be reversed if nobody has the courage to attack its underlying dogmas.

17

Profit and Loss

Entrepreneurs Earn Profits by Anticipating Consumer Wants

In the capitalist system of society's economic organization the entrepreneurs determine the course of production. In the performance of this function they are unconditionally and totally subject to the sovereignty of the buying public, the consumers. If they fail to produce in the cheapest and best possible way those commodities which the consumers are asking for most urgently, they suffer losses and are finally eliminated from their entrepreneurial position. Other men who know better how to serve the consumers replace them.

If all people were to anticipate correctly the future state of the market, the entrepreneurs would neither earn any profits nor suffer any losses. They would have to buy the complementary factors of production at prices which would, already at the instant of the purchase, fully reflect the future prices of the products. No room would be left either for profit or for loss. What makes profit emerge is the fact that the entrepreneur who judges the future prices of the products more correctly than other people do buys some or all of the factors of production at prices which, seen from the point of view of the future state of the market, are too low. Thus the total costs of production—including interest on the capital invested—lag behind the prices which the entrepreneur receives for the product. This difference is entrepreneurial profit.

On the other hand, the entrepreneur who misjudges the future prices of the products allows for the factors of production prices which, seen from the point of view of the future state of the market, are too high. His total costs of production exceed the prices at which he can sell the product. This difference is entrepreneurial loss.

A paper prepared for the meeting of the Mont Pèlerin Society held in Beauvallon, France, September 9 to 16, 1951.

Thus profit and loss are generated by success or failure in adjusting the course of production activities to the most urgent demand of the consumers. Once this adjustment is achieved, they disappear. The prices of the complementary factors of production reach a height at which total costs of production coincide with the price of the product. Profit and loss are ever-present features only on account of the fact that ceaseless change in the economic data makes again and again new discrepancies, and consequently the need for new adjustments originate.

The Entrepreneur Is an Enterprise's Decisionmaker

Many errors concerning the nature of profit and loss were caused by the practice of applying the term profit to the totality of the residual proceeds of an entrepreneur.

Interest on the capital employed is not a component part of profit. The dividends of a corporation are not profit. They are interest on the capital invested plus profit or minus loss.

The market equivalent of work performed by the entrepreneur in the conduct of the enterprise's affairs is entrepreneurial quasi-wages but not profit.

If the enterprise owns a factor on which it can earn monopoly prices, it makes a monopoly gain. If this enterprise is a corporation, such gains increase the dividend. Yet they are not profit proper.

Still more serious are the errors due to the confusion of entrepreneurial activity and technological innovation and improvement.

The maladjustment, the removal of which is the essential function of entrepreneurship, may often consist in the fact that new technological methods have not yet been utilized to the full extent to which they should be in order to bring about the best possible satisfaction of consumers' demand. But this is not necessarily always the case. Changes in the data, especially in consumers' demand, may require adjustments which have no reference at all to technological innovations and improvements. The entrepreneur who simply increases the production of an article by adding to the existing production facilities a new outfit without any change in the technological method of production is no less an entrepreneur than the man who inaugurates a new way of producing. The business of the entrepreneur is not merely to experiment with new technological methods, but to select from the multitude of technologically feasible methods those which are best fit to supply the public in the cheapest way with the things they are asking for most urgently. Whether a new technological procedure is or is not fit for this purpose is to be provisionally decided by the entrepreneur and will be finally decided by the conduct of the buying public. The question is not whether a new method is to be considered as a more "elegant" solution of a technological problem. It is whether, under the given state of economic data, it is the best possible method of supplying the consumers in the cheapest way.

The activities of the entrepreneur consist in making decisions. He determines for what purpose the factors of production should be employed. Any other acts which an entrepreneur may perform are merely accidental to his entrepreneurial function. It is this that laymen often fail to realize. They confuse the entrepreneurial activities with the conduct of the technological and administrative affairs of a plant. In their eyes not the stockholders, the promoters and speculators, but hired employees are the real entrepreneurs. The former are merely idle parasites who pocket the dividends.

Now nobody ever contended that one could produce without working. But neither is it possible to produce without capital goods, the previously produced factors of further production. These capital goods are scarce, i.e., they do not suffice for the production of all things which one would like to have produced. Hence the economic problem arises: to employ them in such a way that only those goods should be produced which are fit to satisfy the most urgent demands of the consumers. No good should remain unproduced on account of the fact that the factors required for its production were used—wasted— for the production of another good for which the demand of the public is less intense. To achieve this is, under capitalism, the function of entrepreneurship that determines the allocation of capital to the various branches of production. Under socialism it would be a function of the state, the social apparatus of coercion and oppression. The problem whether a socialist directorate, lacking any method of economic calculation, could fulfill this function is not to be dealt with in this essay.

There is a simple rule of thumb to tell entrepreneurs from non-entrepreneurs. The entrepreneurs are those on whom the incidence of losses on the capital employed falls. Amateur-economists may confuse profits with other kinds of intakes. But it is impossible to fail to recognize losses on the capital employed.

Government Is Necessary to Preserve and Protect

What has been called the democracy of the market manifests itself in the fact that profit-seeking business is unconditionally subject to the supremacy of the buying public.

Non-profit organizations are sovereign unto themselves. They are, within the limits drawn by the amount of capital at their disposal, in a position to defy the wishes of the public.

A special case is that of the conduct of government affairs, the administration of the social apparatus of coercion and oppression, viz., the police power. The objectives of government, the protection of the inviolability of the individuals' lives and health and of their efforts to improve the material conditions of their existence, are indispensable. They benefit all and are the necessary prerequisite of social cooperation and civilization. But they cannot be sold and bought in the way merchandise is sold and bought; they have therefore no price on the market. With regard to them there cannot be any economic calculation. The costs expended for their conduct cannot be confronted with a price received for the product. This state of affairs would make the officers entrusted with the administration of governmental activities irresponsible despots if they were not curbed by the budget system. Under this system the administrators are forced to comply with detailed instructions enjoined upon them by the sovereign, be it a self-appointed autocrat or the whole people acting through elected representatives. To the officers limited funds are assigned which they are bound to spend only for those purposes which the sovereign has ordered. Thus the management of public administration becomes bureaucratic, i.e., dependent on definite detailed rules and regulations.

Bureaucratic management is the only alternative available where there is no profit and loss management.*

On the Market, Consumers Are Sovereign

The consumers by their buying and abstention from buying elect the entrepreneurs in a daily repeated plebiscite as it were. They determine who should own and who not, and how much each owner should own.

---

* Cf. Mises, *Human Action*, Yale University Press, 1949, pages 305–7 [Auburn, Ala.: Ludwig von Mises Institute, 1998; Indianapolis: Liberty Fund, 2007]; *Bureaucracy*, Yale University Press, 1944, pages 40–73 [Grove City, Pa.: Libertarian Press, 1996; Indianapolis: Liberty Fund, 2007].

As is the case with all acts of choosing a person—choosing holders of public office, employees, friends or a consort—the decision of the consumers is made on the ground of experience and thus necessarily always refers to the past. There is no experience of the future. The ballot of the market elevates those who in the immediate past have best served the consumers. However, the choice is not unalterable and can daily be corrected. The elected who disappoints the electorate is speedily reduced to the ranks.

Each ballot of the consumers adds only a little to the elected man's sphere of action. To reach the upper levels of entrepreneurship he needs a great number of votes, repeated again and again over a long period of time, a protracted series of successful strokes. He must stand every day a new trial, must submit anew to reelection as it were.

It is the same with his heirs. They can retain their eminent position only by receiving again and again confirmation on the part of the public. Their office is revocable. If they retain it, it is not on account of the deserts of their predecessor, but on account of their own ability to employ the capital for the best possible satisfaction of the consumers.

The entrepreneurs are neither perfect nor good in any metaphysical sense. They owe their position exclusively to the fact that they are better fit for the performance of the functions incumbent upon them than other people are. They earn profit not because they are clever in performing their tasks, but because they are more clever or less clumsy than other people are. They are not infallible and often blunder. But they are less liable to error and blunder less than other people do. Nobody has the right to take offense at the errors made by the entrepreneurs in the conduct of affairs and to stress the point that people would have been better supplied if the entrepreneurs had been more skillful and prescient. If the grumbler knew better, why did he not himself fill the gap and seize the opportunity to earn profits? It is easy indeed to display foresight after the event. In retrospect all fools become wise.

A popular chain of reasoning runs this way: The entrepreneur earns profit not only on account of the fact that other people were less successful than he in anticipating correctly the future state of the market. He himself contributed to the emergence of profit by not producing more of the article concerned; but for intentional restriction of output on his part, the supply of this article would have been so ample that the price would have dropped to a point at which no surplus of proceeds over costs of production expended would have emerged. This reasoning is at the bottom of the spurious doctrines of imperfect and monopolistic competition. It was resorted to a short time ago by the American administration when it blamed the enterprises of the steel industry for the fact that the steel production capacity of the United States was not greater than it really was.

Certainly those engaged in the production of steel are not responsible for the fact that other people did not likewise enter this field of production. The reproach on the part of the authorities would have been sensible if they had conferred on the existing steel corporations the monopoly of steel production. But in the absence of such a privilege, the reprimand given to the operating mills is not more justified than it would be to censure the nation's poets and musicians for the fact that there are not more and better poets and musicians. If somebody is to blame for the fact that the number of people who joined the voluntary civilian defense organization is not larger, then it is not those who have already joined but only those who have not.

Capital and Factors of Production Are Limited

That the production of a commodity p is not larger than it really is, is due to the fact that the complementary factors of production required for an expansion were employed for the production of other commodities. To speak of an insufficiency of the supply of p is empty rhetoric if it does not indicate the various products m which were produced in too large quantities with the effect that their production appears now, i.e., after the event, as a waste of scarce factors of production. We may assume that the entrepreneurs who instead of producing additional quantities of p turned to the production of excessive amounts of m and consequently suffered losses did not intentionally make their mistake.

Neither did the producers of p intentionally restrict the production of p. Every entrepreneur's capital is limited; he employs it for those projects which, he expects, will, by filling the most urgent demand of the public, yield the highest profit.

An entrepreneur at whose disposal are 100 units of capital employs, for instance, 50 units for the production of p and 50 units for the production of q. If both lines are profitable, it is odd to blame him for not having employed more, e.g., 75 units, for the production of p. He could increase the production of p only by curtailing correspondingly the production of q. But with regard to q the same fault could be found by the grumblers. If one blames the entrepreneur for not having produced more p, one must blame him also for not having produced more q. This means: one blames the entrepreneur for the facts that there is a scarcity of the factors of production and that the earth is not a land of Cockaigne.

Perhaps the grumbler will object on the ground that he considers p a vital commodity, much more important than q, and that therefore the production of p should be expanded and that of q restricted. If this is really the meaning of his criticism, he is at variance with the valuations of the consumers. He throws off his mask and shows his dictatorial aspirations. Production should not be directed by the wishes of the public but by his own despotic discretion.

But if our entrepreneur's production of q involves a loss, it is obvious that his fault was poor foresight and not intentional.

Entrance into the ranks of the entrepreneurs in a market society, not sabotaged by the interference of government or other agencies resorting to violence, is open to everybody. Those who know how to take advantage of any business opportunity cropping up will always find the capital required. For the market is always full of capitalists anxious to find the most promising employment for their funds and in search of the ingenious newcomers, in partnership with whom they could execute the most remunerative projects.

People often failed to realize this inherent feature of capitalism because they did not grasp the meaning and the effects of capital scarcity. The task of the entrepreneur is to select from the multitude of technologically feasible projects those which will satisfy the most urgent of the not yet satisfied needs of the public. Those projects for the execution of which the capital supply does not suffice must not be carried out. The market is always crammed with visionaries who want to float such impracticable and unworkable schemes. It is these dreamers who always complain about the blindness of the capitalists who are too stupid to look after their own interests. Of course, the investors often err in the choice of their investments. But these faults consist precisely in the fact that they preferred an unsuitable project to another that would have satisfied more urgent needs of the buying public.

Entrepreneurs Follow Consumers When Deciding What to Produce

People often err very lamentably in estimating the work of the creative genius. Only a minority of men are appreciative enough to attach the right value to the achievement of poets, artists and thinkers. It may happen that the indifference of his contemporaries makes it impossible for a genius to accomplish what he would have accomplished if his fellow-men had displayed better judgment. The way in which the poet laureate and the philosopher à la mode are selected is certainly questionable.

But it is impermissible to question the free market's choice of the entrepreneurs. The consumers' preference for definite articles may be open to condemnation from the point of view of a philosopher's judgment. But judgments of value are necessarily always personal and subjective. The consumer chooses what, as he thinks, satisfies him best. Nobody is called upon to determine what could make another man happier or less unhappy. The popularity of motor cars, television sets and nylon stockings may be criticized from a "higher" point of view. But these are the things that people are asking for. They cast their ballots for those entrepreneurs who offer them this merchandise of the best quality at the cheapest price.

In choosing between various political parties and programs for the commonwealth's social and economic organization most people are uninformed and groping in the dark. The average voter lacks the insight to distinguish between policies suitable to attain the ends he is aiming at and those unsuitable. He is at a loss to examine the long chains of aprioristic reasoning which constitute the philosophy of a comprehensive social program. He may at best form some opinion about the short-run effects of the policies concerned. He is helpless in dealing with the long-run effects. The socialists and communists in principle often assert the infallibility of majority decisions. However, they belie their own words in criticizing parliamentary majorities rejecting their creed, and in denying to the people, under the one-party system, the opportunity to choose between different parties.

But in buying a commodity or abstaining from its purchase there is nothing else involved than the consumer's longing for the best possible satisfaction of his instantaneous wishes. The consumer does not—like the voter in political voting—choose between different means whose effects appear only later. He chooses between things which immediately provide satisfaction. His decision is final.

An entrepreneur earns profit by serving the consumers, the people, as they are and not as they should be according to the fancies of some grumbler or potential dictator.

Entrepreneurs Earn Profits by Removing Maladjustments

Profits are never normal. They appear only where there is a maladjustment, a divergence between actual production and production as it should be in order to utilize the available material and mental resources for the best possible satisfaction of the wishes of the public. They are the prize of those who remove this maladjustment; they disappear as soon as the maladjustment is entirely removed. In the imaginary construction of an evenly rotating economy there are no profits. There the sum of the prices of the complementary factors of production, due allowance being made for time preference, coincides with the price of the product.

The greater the preceding maladjustments, the greater the profit earned by their removal. Maladjustments may sometimes be called excessive. But it is inappropriate to apply the epithet "excessive" to profits.

People arrive at the idea of excessive profits by confronting the profit earned with the capital employed in the enterprise and measuring the profit as a percentage of the capital. This method is suggested by the customary procedure applied in partnerships and corporations for the assignment of quotas of the total profit to the individual partners and shareholders. These men have contributed to a different extent to the realization of the project and share in the profits and losses according to the extent of their contribution.

But it is not the capital employed that creates profits and losses. Capital does not "beget profit" as Marx thought. The capital goods as such are dead things that in themselves do not accomplish anything. If they are utilized according to a good idea, profit results. If they are utilized according to a mistaken idea, no profit or losses result. It is the entrepreneurial decision that creates either profit or loss. It is mental acts, the mind of the entrepreneur, from which profits ultimately originate. Profit is a product of the mind, of success in anticipating the future state of the market. It is a spiritual and intellectual phenomenon.

The absurdity of condemning any profits as excessive can easily be shown. An enterprise with a capital of the amount c produced a definite quantity of p which it sold at prices that brought a surplus of proceeds over costs of s and consequently a profit of n per cent. If the entrepreneur had been less capable, he would have needed a capital of $2c$ for the production of the same quantity of p. For the sake of argument we may even neglect the fact that this would have necessarily increased costs of production as it would have doubled the interest on the capital employed, and we may assume that s would have remained unchanged. But at any rate s would have been confronted with 2c instead of c and thus the profit would have been only n/2 per cent of the capital employed. The "excessive" profit would have been reduced to a "fair" level. Why? Because the entrepreneur was less efficient and because his lack of efficiency deprived his fellow-men of all the advantages they could have got if an amount c of capital goods had been left available for the production of other merchandise.

Profits Transfer Capital to Those Who Serve the Public Best

In branding profits as excessive and penalizing the efficient entrepreneurs by discriminatory taxation, people are injuring themselves. Taxing profits is tantamount to taxing success in best serving the public. The only goal of all production activities is to employ the factors of production in such a way that they render the highest possible output. The smaller the input required for the production of an article becomes, the more of the scarce factors of production is left for the production of other articles. But the better an entrepreneur succeeds in this regard, the more is he vilified and the more is he soaked by taxation. Increasing costs per unit of output, that is, waste, is praised as a virtue.

The most amazing manifestation of this complete failure to grasp the task of production and the nature and functions of profit and loss is shown in the popular superstition that profit is an addendum to the costs of production, the height of which depends uniquely on the discretion of the seller. It is this belief that guides governments in controlling prices. It is the same belief that has prompted many governments to make arrangements with their contractors according to which the price to be paid for an article delivered is to equal costs of production expended by the seller increased by a definite percentage. The effect was that the purveyor got a surplus the higher, the less he succeeded in avoiding superfluous costs. Contracts of this type enhanced considerably the sums the United States had to expend in the two world wars. But the bureaucrats, first of all the professors of economics who served in the various war agencies, boasted of their clever handling of the matter.

All people, entrepreneurs as well as non-entrepreneurs, look askance upon any profits earned by other people. Envy is a common weakness of men. People are loath to acknowledge the fact that they themselves could have earned profits if they had displayed the same foresight and judgment the successful businessman did. Their resentment is the more violent the more they are subconsciously aware of this fact.

There would not be any profits but for the eagerness of the public to acquire the merchandise offered for sale by the successful entrepreneur. But the same people who scramble for these articles vilify the businessman and call his profit ill got.

The semantic expression of this enviousness is the distinction between earned and unearned income. It permeates the textbooks, the language of the laws and administrative procedure. Thus, for instance, the official Form 201 for the New York state income tax return calls "earnings" only the compensation received by employees and, by implication, all other income, also that resulting from the exercise of a profession, unearned income. Such is the terminology of a state whose governor is a Republican and whose state assembly has a Republican majority.

Public opinion condones profits only as far as they do not exceed the salary paid to an employee. All surplus is rejected as unfair. The objective of taxation is, under the ability-to-pay principle, to confiscate this surplus.

Now one of the main functions of profits is to shift the control of capital to those who know how to employ it in the best possible way for the satisfaction of the public. The more profits a man earns, the greater his wealth consequently becomes, the more influential does he become in the conduct of business affairs. Profit and loss are the instruments by means of which the consumers pass the direction of production activities into the hands of those who are best fit to serve them. Whatever is undertaken to curtail or to confiscate profits impairs this function. The result of such measures is to loosen the grip the consumers hold over the course of production. The economic machine becomes, from the point of view of the people, less efficient and less responsive.

The jealousy of the common man looks upon the profits of the entrepreneurs as if they were totally used for consumption. A part of them is, of course, consumed. But only those entrepreneurs attain wealth and influence in the realm of business who consume merely a fraction of their proceeds and plough back the much greater part into their enterprises. What makes small business develop into big business is not spending, but saving and capital accumulation.

Profits Exceed Losses in a Progressing Economy

We call a stationary economy an economy in which the per head quota of the income and wealth of the individuals remains unchanged. In such an economy what the consumers spend more for the purchase of some articles must be equal to what they spend less for other articles. The total amount of the profits earned by one part of the entrepreneurs equals the total amount of losses suffered by other entrepreneurs.

A surplus of the sum of all profits earned in the whole economy above the sum of all losses suffered emerges only in a progressing economy, that is, in an economy in which the per head quota of capital increases. This increment is an effect of saving that adds new capital goods to the quantity already previously available. The increase of capital available creates maladjustments insofar as it brings about a discrepancy between the actual state of production and that state which the additional capital makes possible. Thanks to the emergence of additional capital, certain projects which hitherto could not be executed become feasible. In directing the new capital into those channels in which it satisfies the most urgent among the previously not satisfied wants of the consumers, the entrepreneurs earn profits which are not counterbalanced by the losses of other entrepreneurs.

The enrichment which the additional capital generates goes only in part to those who have created it by saving. The rest goes, by raising the marginal productivity of labor and thereby wage rates, to the earners of wages and salaries and, by raising the prices of definite raw materials and foodstuffs, to the owners of land, and, finally, to the entrepreneurs who integrate this new capital into the most economical production processes. But while the gain of the wage earners and of the landowners is permanent, the profits of the entrepreneurs disappear once this integration is accomplished. Profits of the entrepreneurs are, as has been mentioned already, a permanent phenomenon only on account of the fact that maladjustments appear daily anew by the elimination of which profits are earned.

Let us for the sake of argument resort to the concept of national income as employed in popular economics. Then it is obvious that in a stationary economy no part of the national income goes into profits. Only in a progressing economy is there a surplus of total profits over total losses. The popular belief that profits are a deduction from the income of workers and consumers is entirely fallacious. If we want to apply the term deduction to the issue, we have to say that this surplus of profits over losses as well as the increments of the wage earners and the landowners is deducted from the gains of those whose saving brought about the additional capital. It is their saving that is the vehicle of economic improvment, that makes the employment of technological innovations possible and raises productivity and the standard of living. It is the entrepreneurs whose activity takes care of the most economical employment of the additional capital. As far as they themselves do not save, neither the workers nor the landowners contribute anything to the emergence of the circumstances which generate what is called economic progress and improvement. They are benefited by other peoples' saving that creates additional capital on the one hand and by the entrepreneurial action that directs this additional capital toward the satisfaction of the most urgent wants on the other hand.

A retrogressing economy is an economy in which the per head quota of capital invested is decreasing. In such an economy the total amount of losses incurred by entrepreneurs exceeds the total amount of profits earned by other entrepreneurs.

Expressing Profits in Monetary Terms Can Cause Problems

The originary praxeological categories of profit and loss are psychic qualities and not reducible to any interpersonal description in quantitative terms. They are intensive magnitudes. The difference between the value of the end attained and that of the means applied for its attainment is profit if it is positive and loss if it is negative.

Where there are social division of efforts and cooperation as well as private ownership of the means of production, economic calculation in terms of monetary units becomes feasible and necessary. Profit and loss are computable as social phenomena. The psychic phenomena of profit and loss, from which they are ultimately derived, remain, of course, incalculable intensive magnitudes.

The fact that in the frame of the market economy entrepreneurial profit and loss are determined by arithmetical operations has misled many people. They fail to see that essential items that enter into this calculation are estimates emanating from the entrepreneur's specific understanding of the future state of the market. They think that these computations are open to examination and verification or alteration on the part of a disinterested expert. They ignore the fact that such computations are as a rule an inherent part of the entrepreneur's speculative anticipation of uncertain future conditions.

For the task of this essay it suffices to refer to one of the problems of cost accounting. One of the items of a bill of costs is the establishment of the difference between the price paid for the acquisition of what is commonly called durable production equipment and its present value. This present value is the money equivalent of the contribution this equipment will make to future earnings. There is no certainty about the future state of the market and about the height of these earnings. They can only be determined by a speculative anticipation on the part of the entrepreneur. It is preposterous to call in an expert and to substitute his arbitrary judgment for that of the entrepreneur. The expert is objective insofar as he is not affected by an error made. But the entrepreneur exposes his own material well-being.

Of course, the law determines magnitudes which it calls profit and loss. But these magnitudes are not identical with the economic concepts of profit and loss and must not be confused with them. If a tax law calls a magnitude profit, it in effect determines the height of taxes due. It calls this magnitude profit because it wants to justify its tax policy in the eyes of the public. It would be more correct for the legislator to omit the term profit and simply to speak of the basis for the computation of the tax due.

The tendency of the tax laws is to compute what they call profit as high as possible in order to increase immediate public revenue. But there are other laws which are committed to the tendency to restrict the magnitude they call profit. The commercial codes of many nations were and are guided by the endeavor to protect the rights of creditors. They aimed at restricting what they called profit in order to prevent the entrepreneur from withdrawing to the prejudice of creditors too much from the firm or corporation for his own benefit. It was these tendencies which were operative in the evolution of the commercial usages concerning the customary height of depreciation quotas.

There is no need today to dwell upon the problem of the falsification of economic calculation under inflationary conditions. All people begin to comprehend the phenomenon of illusory profits, the offshoot of the great inflations of our age.

Failure to grasp the effects of inflation upon the customary methods of computing profits originated the modern concept of *profiteering*. An entrepreneur is dubbed a profiteer if his profit and loss statement, calculated in terms of a currency subject to a rapidly progressing inflation, shows profits which other people deem "excessive." It has happened very often in many countries that the profit and loss statement of such a profiteer, when calculated in terms of a non-inflated or less inflated currency, showed not only no profit at all but considerable losses.

Even if we neglect for the sake of argument any reference to the phenomenon of merely inflation-induced illusory profits, it is obvious that the epithet profiteer is the expression of an arbitrary judgment of value. There is no other standard available for the distinction between profiteering and earning fair profits than that provided by the censor's personal envy and resentment.

Logician Distinguishes "Legitimate" from "Illegitimate" Profits

It is strange indeed that an eminent logician, the late L. Susan Stebbing, entirely failed to perceive the issue involved. Professor Stebbing equated the concept of profiteering to concepts which refer to a clear distinction of such a nature that no sharp line can be drawn between extremes. The distinction between excess profits or profiteering, and "legitimate profits," she declared, is clear, although it is not a sharp distinction.* Now this distinction is clear only in reference to an act of legislation that defines the term excess profits as used in its context. But this is not what Stebbing had in mind. She explicitly emphasized that such legal definitions are made "in an arbitrary manner for the practical purposes of administration." She used the term *legitimate* without any reference to legal statutes and their definitions. But is it permissible to employ the term legitimate without reference to any standard from the point of view of which the thing in question is to be considered as legitimate? And is there any other standard available for the distinction between profiteering and legitimate profits than one provided by personal judgments of value?

Professor Stebbing referred to the famous *acervus* and *calvus* arguments of the old logicians. Many words are vague insofar as they apply to characteristics which may be possessed in varying degrees. It is impossible to draw a sharp line between those who are bald and those who are not. It is impossible to define precisely the concept of baldness. But what Professor Stebbing failed to notice is that the characteristic

---

* Cf. L. Susan Stebbing, *Thinking to Some Purpose* (Pelican Books A44), pages 185–87.

according to which people distinguish between those who are bald and those who are not is open to a precise definition. It is the presence or the absence of hair on the head of a person. This is a clear and unambiguous mark of which the presence or absence is to be established by observation and to be expressed by propositions about existence. What is vague is merely the determination of the point at which non-baldness turns into baldness. People may disagree with regard to the determination of this point. But their disagreement refers to the interpretation of the convention that attaches a certain meaning to the word baldness. No judgments of value are implied. It may, of course, happen that the difference of opinion is in a concrete case caused by bias. But this is another thing.

The vagueness of words like bald is the same that is inherent in the indefinite numerals and pronouns. Language needs such terms as for many purposes of daily communication between men an exact arithmetical establishment of quantities is superfluous and too bothersome. Logicians are badly mistaken in attempting to attach to such words whose vagueness is intentional and serves definite purposes the precision of the definite numerals. For an individual who plans to visit Seattle the information that there are many hotels in this city is sufficient. A committee that plans to hold a convention in Seattle needs precise information about the number of hotel beds available.

Professor Stebbing's error consisted in the confusion of existential propositions with judgments of value. Her unfamiliarity with the problems of economics, which all her otherwise valuable writings display, led her astray. She would not have made such a blunder in a field that was better known to her. She would not have declared that there is a clear distinction between an author's "legitimate royalties" and "illegitimate royalties." She would have comprehended that the height of the royalties depends on the public's appreciation of a book and that an observer who criticizes the height of royalties merely expresses his personal judgment of value.

Suppose Profits Were Abolished?

Those who spurn entrepreneurial profit as "unearned" mean that it is lucre unfairly withheld either from the workers or from the consumers or from both. Such is the idea underlying the alleged "right to the whole produce of labor" and the Marxian doctrine of exploitation. It can be said that most governments—if not all—and the immense majority of our contemporaries by and large endorse this opinion although some of them are generous enough to acquiesce in the suggestion that a fraction of profits should be left to the "exploiters."

There is no use in arguing about the adequacy of ethical precepts. They are derived from intuition; they are arbitrary and subjective. There is no objective standard available with regard to which they could be judged. Ultimate ends are chosen by the individual's judgments of value. They cannot be determined by scientific inquiry and logical reasoning. If a man says, "This is what I am aiming at whatever the consequences of my conduct and the price I shall have to pay for it may be," nobody is in a position to oppose any arguments against him. But the question is whether it is really true that this man is ready to pay any price for the attainment of the end concerned. If this latter question is answered in the negative, it becomes possible to enter into an examination of the issue involved.

If there were really people who are prepared to put up with all the consequences of the abolition of profit, however detrimental they may be, it would not be possible for economics to deal with the problem. But this is not the case. Those who want to abolish profit are guided by the idea that this confiscation would improve the material well-being of all non-entrepreneurs. In their eyes the abolition of profit is not an ultimate end but a means for the attainment of a definite end, viz., the enrichment of the non-entrepreneurs. Whether this end can really be attained by the employment of this means and whether the employment of this means does not perhaps bring about some other effects which may to some or to all people appear more undesirable than conditions before the employment of this means, these are questions which economics is called upon to examine.

The idea to abolish profit for the advantage of the consumers involves that the entrepreneur should be forced to sell the products at prices not exceeding the costs of production expended. As such prices are, for all articles the sale of which would have brought profit, below the potential market price, the available supply is not sufficient to make it possible for all those who want to buy at these prices to acquire the articles. The market is paralyzed by the maximum price decree. It can no longer allocate the products to the consumers. A system of rationing must be adopted.

The suggestion to abolish the entrepreneur's profit for the benefit of the employees aims not at the abolition of profit. It aims at wresting it from the hands of the entrepreneur and handing it over to his employees.

Under such a scheme the incidence of losses incurred falls upon the entrepreneur, while profits go to the employees. It is probable that the effect of this arrangement would consist in making losses increase and profits dwindle. At any rate, a greater part of the profits would be consumed and less would be saved and ploughed back into the enterprise. No capital would be available for the establishment of new branches of production and for the transfer of capital from branches which—in compliance with the demand of the customers—should shrink into branches which should expand. For it would harm the interests of those employed in a definite enterprise or branch to restrict the capital employed in it and to transfer it into another enterprise or branch. If such a scheme had been adopted half a century ago, all the innovations accomplished in this period would have been rendered impossible. If, for the sake of argument, we were prepared to neglect any reference to the problem of capital accumulation, we would still have to realize that giving profit to the employees must result in rigidity of the once attained state of production and preclude any adjustment, improvement and progress.

In fact, the scheme would transfer ownership of the capital invested into the hands of the employees. It would be tantamount to the establishment of syndicalism and would generate all the effects of syndicalism, a system which no author or reformer ever had the courage to advocate openly.

A third solution of the problem would be to confiscate all the profits earned by the entrepreneurs for the benefit of the state. A one hundred per cent tax on profits would accomplish this task. It would transform the entrepreneurs into irresponsible administrators of all plants and workshops. They would no longer be subject to the supremacy of the buying public. They would just be people who have the power to deal with production as it pleases them.

The policies of all contemporary governments which have not adopted outright socialism apply all these three schemes jointly. They confiscate by various measures of price control a part of the potential profits for the alleged benefit of the consumers. They support the labor unions in their endeavors to wrest, under the ability-to-pay principle of wage determination, a part of the profits from the entrepreneurs. And, last but not least, they are intent upon confiscating, by progressive income taxes, special taxes on corporation income, and "excess profits" taxes, an ever-increasing part of profits for public revenue. It can easily be seen that these policies if continued will very soon succeed in abolishing entrepreneurial profit altogether.

The joint effect of the application of these policies is already today rising chaos. The final effect will be the full realization of socialism by smoking out the entrepreneurs. Capitalism cannot survive the abolition of profit. It is profit and loss that force the capitalists to employ their capital for the best possible service to the consumers. It is profit and loss that make those people supreme in the conduct of business who are best fit to satisfy the public. If profit is abolished, chaos results.

Profits and Losses Guide Entrepreneurs

All the reasons advanced in favor of an anti-profit policy are the outcome of an erroneous interpretation of the operation of the market economy.

The tycoons are too powerful, too rich and too big. They abuse their power for their own enrichment. They are irresponsible tyrants. Bigness of an enterprise is in itself an evil. There is no reason why some men should own millions while others are poor. The wealth of the few is the cause of the poverty of the masses.

Each word of these passionate denunciations is false. The businessmen are not irresponsible tyrants. It is precisely the necessity of making profits and avoiding losses that gives to the consumers a firm hold over the entrepreneurs and forces them to comply with the wishes of the people. What makes a firm big is its success in best filling the demands of the buyers. If the bigger enterprise did not better serve the people than a smaller one, it would long since have been reduced to smallness. There is no harm in a businessman's endeavors to enrich himself by increasing his profits. The businessman has in his capacity as a businessman only one task: to strive after the highest possible profit. Huge profits are the proof of good service rendered in supplying the consumers. Losses are the proof of blunders committed, of failure to perform satisfactorily the tasks incumbent upon an entrepreneur. The riches of successful entrepreneurs are not the cause of anybody's poverty; they are consequences of the fact that the consumers are better supplied than they would have been in the absence of the entrepreneur's effort. The penury of millions in the backward countries is not caused by anybody's opulence; it is the correlative of the fact that their country lacks entrepreneurs who have acquired riches. The standard of living of the common man is highest in those countries which have the greatest number of wealthy entrepreneurs. It is to the foremost material interest of everybody that control of the factors of production should be concentrated in the hands of those who know how to utilize them in the most efficient way.

It is the avowed objective of the policies of all present-day governments and political parties to prevent the emergence of new millionaires. If this policy had been adopted in the United States fifty years ago, the growth of the industries producing new articles would have been stunted. Motorcars, refrigerators, radio sets and a hundred other less spectacular but even more useful innovations would not have become standard equipment of most of the American family households.

The average wage earner thinks that nothing else is needed to keep the social apparatus of production running and to improve and to increase output than the comparatively simple routine work assigned to him. He does not realize that the mere toil and trouble of the routinist is not sufficient. Sedulousness and skill are spent in vain if they are not directed toward the most important goal by the entrepreneur's foresight and are not aided by the capital accumulated by capitalists. The American worker is badly mistaken when he believes that his high standard of living is due to his own excellence. He is neither more industrious nor more skillful than the workers of Western Europe. He owes his superior income to the fact that his country clung to "rugged individualism" much longer than Europe. It was his luck that the United States turned to an anti-capitalistic policy as much as forty or fifty years later than Germany. His wages are higher than those of the workers of the rest of the world because the capital equipment per head of the employee is highest in America and because the American entrepreneur was not so much restricted by crippling regimentation as his colleagues in other areas. The comparatively greater prosperity of the United States is an outcome of the fact that the New Deal did not come in 1900 or 1910, but only in 1933.

If one wants to study the reasons for Europe's backwardness, it would be necessary to examine the manifold laws and regulations that prevented in Europe the establishment of an equivalent of the American drugstore and crippled the evolution of chain stores, department stores, supermarkets and kindred outfits. It would be important to investigate the German Reich's effort to protect the inefficient methods of traditional *Handwerk* (handicraft) against the competition of capitalist business. Still more revealing would be an examination of the Austrian *Gewerbepolitik,* a policy that from the early eighties on aimed at preserving the economic structure of the ages preceding the Industrial Revolution.

The worst menace to prosperity and civilization and to the material well-being of the wage earners is the inability of union bosses, of "union economists" and of the less intelligent strata of the workers themselves to appreciate the role entrepreneurs play in production. This lack of insight has found a classical expression in the writings of Lenin. As Lenin saw it all that production requires besides the manual work of the laborer and the designing of the engineers is "control of production and distribution," a task that can easily be accomplished "by the armed workers." For this accounting and control "have been *simplified* by capitalism to the utmost, till they have become the extraordinarily simple operations of watching, recording and issuing receipts, within the reach of everybody who can read and write and knows the first four rules of arithmetic." * No further comment is needed.

In the eyes of the parties who style themselves progressive and leftist the main vice of capitalism is the inequality of incomes and wealth. The ultimate end of their policies is to establish equality. The moderates want to attain this goal step by step; the radicals plan to attain it at one stroke, by a revolutionary overthrow of the capitalist mode of production.

However, in talking about equality and asking vehemently for its realization, nobody advocates a curtailment of his own present income. The term equality as employed in contemporary political language always means upward levelling of one's income, never downward levelling. It means getting more, not sharing one's own affluence with people who have less.

If the American automobile worker, railroadman or compositor says equality, he means expropriating the holders of shares and bonds for

---

* Lenin, *State and Revolution,* 1917 (Edition by International Publishers, New York, pages 83–84). The italics are Lenin's (or the communist translator's).

his own benefit. He does not consider sharing with the unskilled workers who earn less. At best, he thinks of equality of all American citizens. It never occurs to him that the peoples of Latin America, Asia and Africa may interpret the postulate of equality as world equality and not as national equality.

Worldwide Income Equalization Would Damage
the International Capital Market

The political labor movement as well as the labor union movement flamboyantly advertise their internationalism. But this internationalism is a mere rhetorical gesture without any substantial meaning. In every country in which average wage rates are higher than in any other area, the unions advocate insurmountable immigration barriers in order to prevent foreign "comrades" and "brothers" from competing with their own members. Compared with the anti-immigration laws of the European nations, the immigration legislation of the American republics is mild indeed because it permits the immigration of a limited number of people. No such normal quotas are provided in most of the European laws.

All the arguments advanced in favor of income equalization within a country can with the same justification or lack of justification also be advanced in favor of world equalization. An American worker has no better title to claim the savings of the American capitalist than has any foreigner. That a man has earned profits by serving the consumers and has not entirely consumed his funds but ploughed back the greater part of them into industrial equipment does not give anybody a valid title to expropriate this capital for his own benefit. But if one maintains the opinion to the contrary, there is certainly no reason to ascribe to anybody a better right to expropriate than to anybody else. There is no reason to assert that only Americans have the right to expropriate other Americans. The big shots of American business are the scions of people who immigrated to the United States from England, Scotland, Ireland, France, Germany and other European countries. The people of their country of origin contend that they have the same title to seize the property acquired by these men as the American people have. The American radicals are badly mistaken in believing that their social program is identical or at least compatible with the objectives of the radicals of other countries. It is not. The foreign radicals will not acquiesce in leaving to the Americans, a minority of less than seven per cent of the world's total population, what they think is a privileged position. A world government of the kind the American radicals are asking for would try to confiscate by a world income tax all the surplus an average American earns above the average income of a Chinese or Indian worker. Those who question the correctness of this statement would drop their doubts after a conversation with any of the intellectual leaders of Asia.

There is hardly any Iranian who would qualify the objections raised by the British Labor government against the confiscation of the oil wells as anything else but a manifestation of the most reactionary spirit of capitalist exploitation. Today governments abstain from virtually expropriating—by foreign exchange control, discriminatory taxation and similar devices—foreign investments only if they expect to get in the next years more foreign capital and thus to be able in the future to expropriate a greater amount.

The disintegration of the international capital market is one of the most important effects of the anti-profit mentality of our age. But no less disastrous is the fact that the greater part of the world's population looks upon the United States—not only upon the American capitalists but also upon the American workers—with the same feelings of envy, hatred and hostility with which, stimulated by the socialist and communist doctrines, the masses everywhere look upon the capitalists of their own nation.

Will Government Programs Achieve Their Goals?

A customary method of dealing with political programs and movements is to explain and to justify their popularity by referring to the conditions which people found unsatisfactory and to the goals they wanted to attain by the realization of these programs.

However, the only thing that matters is whether or not the program concerned is fit to attain the ends sought. A bad program and a bad policy can never be explained, still less justified by pointing to the unsatisfactory conditions of its originators and supporters. The sole question that counts is whether or not these policies can remove or alleviate the evils which they are designed to remedy.

Yet almost all our contemporaries declare again and again: If you want to succeed in fighting communism, socialism and interventionism, you must first of all improve peoples' material conditions. The policy of *laissez faire* aims precisely at making people more prosperous.

But it cannot succeed as long as want is worsened more and more by socialist and interventionist measures.

In the very short run the conditions of a part of the people can be improved by expropriating entrepreneurs and capitalists and by distributing the booty. But such predatory inroads, which even the *Communist Manifesto* described as "despotic" and as "economically insufficient and untenable," sabotage the operation of the market economy, impair very soon the conditions of all the people, and frustrate the endeavors of entrepreneurs and capitalists to make the masses more prosperous. What is good for a quickly vanishing instant, (i.e., in the shortest run) may very soon (i.e., in the long run) result in most detrimental consequences.

Historians are mistaken in explaining the rise of Nazism by referring to real or imaginary adversities and hardships of the German people. What made the Germans support almost unanimously the twenty-five points of the "unalterable" Hitler program was not some conditions which they deemed unsatisfactory, but their expectation that the execution of this program would remove their complaints and render them happier. They turned to Nazism because they lacked common sense and intelligence. They were not judicious enough to recognize in time the disasters that Nazism was bound to bring upon them.

The immense majority of the world's population is extremely poor when compared with the average standard of living of the capitalist nations. But this poverty does not explain their propensity to adopt the communist program. They are anti-capitalistic because they are blinded by envy, ignorant and too dull to appreciate correctly the causes of their distress. There is but one means to improve their material conditions, namely, to convince them that only capitalism can render them more prosperous.

The worst method to fight communism is that of the Marshall Plan. It gives to the recipients the impression that the United States alone is interested in the preservation of the profit system while their own concerns require a communist regime. The United States, they think, is aiding them because its people have a bad conscience. They themselves pocket this bribe but their sympathies go to the socialist system. The American subsidies make it possible for their governments to conceal partially the disastrous effects of the various socialist measures they have adopted.

Not poverty is the source of socialism, but spurious ideological prepossessions. Most of our contemporaries reject beforehand, without having ever studied them, all the teachings of economics as aprioristic nonsense. Only experience, they maintain, is to be relied upon. But is there any experience that would speak in favor of socialism?

Retorts the socialist: But capitalism creates poverty; look at India and China. The objection is vain. Neither India nor China has ever established capitalism. Their poverty is the result of the absence of capitalism.

What happened in these and other underdeveloped countries was that they were benefited from abroad by some of the fruits of capitalism without having adopted the capitalist mode of production. European, and in more recent years also American, capitalists invested capital in their areas and thereby increased the marginal productivity of labor and wage rates. At the same time these peoples received from abroad the means to fight contagious diseases, medications developed in the capitalist countries. Consequently mortality rates, especially infant mortality, dropped considerably. In the capitalist countries this prolongation of the average length of life was partially compensated by a drop in the birth rate. As capital accumulation increased more quickly than population, the per head quota of capital invested grew continuously. The result was progressing prosperity. It was different in the countries which enjoyed some of the effects of capitalism without turning to capitalism. There the birth rate did not decline at all or not to the extent required to make the per head quota of capital invested rise. These nations prevent by their policies both the importation of foreign capital and the accumulation of domestic capital. The joint effect of the high birth rate and the absence of an increase in capital is, of course, increasing poverty.

There is but one means to improve the material well-being of men, viz., to accelerate the increase in capital accumulated as against population. No psychological lucubrations, however sophisticated, can alter this fact. There is no excuse whatever for the pursuit of policies which not only fail to attain the ends sought, but even seriously impair conditions.

As soon as the problem of profits is raised, people shift it from the praxeological sphere into the sphere of ethical judgments of value. Then everybody glories in the aureole of a saint and an ascetic. He himself does not care for money and material well-being. He serves his fellow-men to the best of his abilities unselfishly. He strives after higher and nobler things than wealth. Thank God, he is not one of those egoistic profiteers.

Businessmen Improve Social Cooperation and Economic
Welfare by Earning Profits

The businessmen are blamed because the only thing they have in mind is to succeed. Yet everybody—without any exception—in acting aims at the attainment of a definite end. The only alternative to success is failure; nobody ever wants to fail. It is the very essence of human nature that man consciously aims at substituting a more satisfactory state of affairs for a less satisfactory. What distinguishes the decent man from the crook is the different goals they are aiming at and the different means they are resorting to in order to attain the ends chosen. But they both want to succeed in their sense. It is logically impermissible to distinguish between people who aim at success and those who do not.

Practically everybody aims at improving the material conditions of his existence. Public opinion takes no offense at the endeavors of farmers, workers, clerks, teachers, doctors, ministers, and people from many other callings to earn as much as they can. But it censures the capitalists and entrepreneurs for their greed. While enjoying without any scruples all the goods business delivers, the consumer sharply condemns the selfishness of the purveyors of this merchandise. He does not realize that he himself creates their profits by scrambling for the things they have to sell.

Neither does the average man comprehend that profits are indispensable in order to direct the activities of business into those channels in which they serve him best. He looks upon profits as if their only function were to enable the recipients to consume more than he himself does. He fails to realize that their main function is to convey control of the factors of production into the hands of those who best utilize them for his own purposes. He did not, as he thinks, renounce becoming an entrepreneur out of moral scruples. He chose a position with a more modest yield because he lacked the abilities required for entrepreneurship or, in rare cases indeed, because his inclinations prompted him to enter upon another career.

Mankind ought to be grateful to those exceptional men who out of scientific zeal, humanitarian enthusiasm or religious faith sacrificed their lives, health and wealth, in the service of their fellow-men. But the philistines practice self-deception in comparing themselves with the pioneers of medical X-ray application or with nuns who attend people afflicted with the plague. It is not self-denial that makes the average physician choose a medical career, but the expectation of attaining a respected social position and a suitable income.

Everybody is eager to charge for his services and accomplishments as much as the traffic can bear. In this regard there is no difference between the workers, whether unionized or not, the ministers, and teachers on the one hand and the entrepreneurs on the other hand. Neither of them has the right to talk as if he were Francis d'Assisi.

What Is Morally Good Fosters Social Cooperation

There is no other standard of what is morally good and morally bad than the effects produced by conduct upon social cooperation. A—hypothetical—isolated and self-sufficient individual would not in acting have to take into account anything else than his own well-being. Social man must in all his actions avoid indulging in any conduct that would jeopardize the smooth working of the system of social cooperation. In complying with the moral law man does not sacrifice his own concerns to those of a mythical higher entity, whether it is called class, state, nation, race or humanity. He curbs some of his own instinctive urges, appetites and greed, that is his short-run concerns, in order to serve best his own—rightly understood or long-run—interests. He foregoes a small gain that he could reap instantly lest he miss a greater but later satisfaction. For the attainment of all human ends, whatever they may be, is conditioned by the preservation and further development of social bonds and interhuman cooperation. What is an indispensable means to intensify social cooperation and to make it possible for more people to survive and to enjoy a higher standard of living is morally good and socially desirable. Those who reject this principle as un-Christian ought to ponder over the text: "That thy days may be long upon the land which the Lord thy God giveth thee." They can certainly not deny that capitalism has made man's days longer than they were in the precapitalistic ages.

There is no reason why capitalists and entrepreneurs should be ashamed of earning profits. It is silly that some people try to defend American capitalism by declaring: "The record of American business is good; profits are not too high." The function of entrepreneurs is to make profits; high profits are the proof that they have well performed their task of removing maladjustments of production.

Of course, as a rule capitalists and entrepreneurs are not saints excelling in the virtue of self-denial. But neither are their critics saintly. And with all the regard due to the sublime self-effacement of saints, we cannot help stating the fact that the world would be in a rather desolate condition if it were peopled exclusively by men not interested in the pursuit of material well-being.

Socialists Ignore the Role of Change and Entrepreneurial Decisions in Producing and Creating Wealth

The average man lacks the imagination to realize that the conditions of life and action are in a continual flux. As he sees it, there is no change in the external objects that constitute his well-being. His world view is static and stationary. It mirrors a stagnating environment. He knows neither that the past differed from the present nor that there prevails uncertainty about future things. He is at a complete loss to conceive the function of entrepreneurship because he is unaware of this uncertainty. Like children who take all the things the parents give them without asking any questions, he takes all the goods business offers him. He is unaware of the efforts that supply him with all he needs. He ignores the role of capital accumulation and of entrepreneurial decisions. He simply takes it for granted that a magic table appears at a moment's notice laden with all he wants to enjoy.

This mentality is reflected in the popular idea of socialization. Once the parasitic capitalists and entrepreneurs are thrown out, he himself will get all that they used to consume. It is but the minor error of this expectation that it grotesquely overrates the increment in income, if any, each individual could receive from such a distribution. Much more serious is the fact that it assumes that the only thing required is to continue in the various plants production of those goods they are producing at the moment of the socialization in the ways they were hitherto produced. No account is taken of the necessity to adjust production daily anew to perpetually changing conditions. The dilettante-socialist does not comprehend that a socialization effected fifty years ago would not have socialized the structure of business as it exists today but a very different structure. He does not give a thought to the enormous effort that is needed in order to transform business again and again to render the best possible service.

This dilettantish inability to comprehend the essential issues of the conduct of production affairs is not only manifested in the writings of

Marx and Engels. It permeates no less the contributions of contemporary pseudo-economics.

The imaginary construction of an evenly rotating economy is an indispensable mental tool of economic thinking. In order to conceive the function of profit and loss, the economist constructs the image of a hypothetical, although unrealizable, state of affairs in which nothing changes, in which tomorrow does not differ at all from today, and in which consequently no maladjustments can arise and no need for any alteration in the conduct of business emerges. In the frame of this imaginary construction there are no entrepreneurs and no entrepreneurial profits and losses. The wheels turn spontaneously, as it were. But the real world in which men live and have to work can never duplicate the hypothetical world of this mental makeshift.

Now one of the main shortcomings of the mathematical economists is that they deal with this evenly rotating economy—they call it the static state—as if it were something really existing. Prepossessed by the fallacy that economics is to be treated with mathematical methods, they concentrate their efforts upon the analysis of static states which, of course, allow a description in sets of simultaneous differential equations. But this mathematical treatment virtually avoids any reference to the real problems of economics. It indulges in quite useless mathematical play without adding anything to the comprehension of the problems of human acting and producing. It creates the misunderstanding as if the analysis of static states were the main concern of economics. It confuses a merely ancillary tool of thinking with reality.

The mathematical economist is so blinded by his epistemological prejudice that he simply fails to see what the tasks of economics are. He is anxious to show us that socialism is realizable under static conditions. As static conditions, as he himself admits, are unrealizable, this amounts merely to the assertion that in an unrealizable state of the world socialism would be realizable. A very valuable result, indeed, of a hundred years of the joint work of hundreds of authors, taught at all universities, publicized in innumerable textbooks and monographs and in scores of allegedly scientific magazines!

There is no such thing as a static economy. All the conclusions derived from preoccupation with the image of static states and static equilibrium are of no avail for the description of the world as it is and will always be.

Men Must Choose Capitalism or Socialism: There Is No Middle Way

A social order based on private control of the means of production cannot work without entrepreneurial action and entrepreneurial profit and, of course, entrepreneurial loss. The elimination of profit, whatever methods may be resorted to for its execution, must transform society into a senseless jumble. It would create poverty for all.

In a socialist system there are neither entrepreneurs nor entrepreneurial profit and loss. The supreme director of the socialist commonwealth would, however, have to strive in the same way after a surplus of proceeds over costs as the entrepreneurs do under capitalism. It is not the task of this essay to deal with socialism. Therefore it is not necessary to stress the point that, not being able to apply any kind of economic calculation, the socialist chief would never know what the costs and what the proceeds of his operations are.

What matters in this context is merely the fact that there is no third system feasible. There cannot be any such thing as a non-socialist system without entrepreneurial profit and loss. The endeavors to eliminate profits from the capitalist system are merely destructive. They disintegrate capitalism without putting anything in its place. It is this that we have in mind in maintaining that they result in chaos.

Men must choose between capitalism and socialism. They cannot avoid this dilemma by resorting to a capitalist system without entrepreneurial profit. Every step toward the elimination of profit is progress on the way toward social disintegration.

In choosing between capitalism and socialism people are implicitly also choosing between all the social institutions which are the necessary accompaniment of each of these systems, its "superstructure" as Marx said. If control of production is shifted from the hands of entrepreneurs, daily anew elected by a plebiscite of the consumers, into the hands of the supreme commander of the "industrial armies" (Marx and Engels) or of the "armed workers" (Lenin), neither representative government nor any civil liberties can survive. Wall Street, against which the self-styled idealists are battling, is merely a symbol. But the walls of the Soviet prisons within which all dissenters disappear forever are a hard fact.

INDEX

agricultural prices, x, 43–44, 58–59,
135–36
American Academy of Political and
Social Science, 33–34
Anderson, Benjamin McAlester, 90–94,
119
anti-business ideology, 131
anti-capitalism, 30–32, 41, 51–52, 134–35
"Are Taxes Too High?" (Groves), 34
Ashton, T. S., 131
automatic planning, as false choice,
21–22

baldness analogy, 157–58
Beveridge, William, 3, 62
Bismarck, Otto von, 4, 88
Böhm-Bawerk, Eugen von, ixn2
Bretano, Lujo, 23
bureaucracy: as economic valuation
alternative, 146; Germany's, 57; self-
interests, 23–24; and socialism, 5; and
university teachings, 129–30

Cairnes, J. E., 18–21
Capital and Interest (Böhm-Bawerk),
ixn2
capitalism: Marxist perspectives, 85–88,
111; socialism's perspective, 41–43;
university teachings, 130–32; unpopu-
larity, 30–32, 41, 51–52, 134–35
capital supply: cheap money myth,
78–79; and government spending
myth, 65–66; from human attention,
123–24; living standards, 27–30, 70,

74–75, 80–81; pensions, 66–67; and
productivity, 25–26; profits, 152–53,
160, 161, 164–65; in progressing
economy, 154–55; scarcity factors,
34–35; taxation, 33–34, 50; wages, 10,
34, 37, 69, 74–75
catallactics, 120
cheap-money myth, 77–78
Clemenceau, Georges, 8, 105
Cole, G. D. H., 15–16
commodity characterization, 8–9
Communist Manifesto (Marx and Engels), 48, 49, 50, 86, 87–89, 114, 137
conscious planning, as false choice,
21–22
The Constitution of Liberty (Hayek), 113
Constitutions, 127–28
consumers: as common man, 13–14,
131–32; in market economy, x, 22,
53–54; role in profits, 12–13, 146–47,
149–50, 161; role in wages, 68, 79–80;
in socialism, 5, 47
cost accounting systems, 156–57
credit expansion: Anderson's criticisms,
91–92; cheap money myth, 78–79; and
depression, 7–8, 47, 79, 97–98; and
living standards, 6; and wages, 11–12,
70–71
Cripps, Stafford, 94

Das Kapital (Marx), 48
deficit spending, 11, 57, 63–65, 77. *See
also* credit expansion
depreciation, 34

The typeface used in setting this book is Electra, designed in 1935 by the great American typographer William Addison Dwiggins. Dwiggins was a student and associate of Frederic Goudy and served for a time as acting director of Harvard University Press. In his illustrious career as typographer and book designer (he coined the term "graphic designer"), Dwiggins created a number of typefaces, including Metro and Caledonia, and designed as well many of the typographic ornaments or "dingbats" familiar to readers.

Electra is a crisp, elegant, and readable typeface, strongly suggestive of calligraphy. The contrast between its strokes is relatively muted, and it produces an even but still "active" impression in text. Interestingly, the design of the *italic* form—called "cursive" in this typeface—is less calligraphic than the italic form of many faces, and more closely resembles the roman.

This book is printed on paper that is acid-free and meets the requirements of the American National Standard for Permanence of Paper for Printed Library Materials, z39.48–1992. ∞

Book design adapted by Erin Kirk New, Watkinsville, Georgia, after a design by Martin Lubin Graphic Design, Jackson Heights, New York

Typography by Newgen

Printed and bound by Worzalla, Stevens Point, Wisconsin